A Poet's Guide to Britain

A Poet's Guide to Britain

Selected with an Introduction by
OWEN SHEERS

PENGUIN CLASSICS
an imprint of
PENGUIN BOOKS

PENGUIN CLASSICS

Published by the Penguin Group
Penguin Books Ltd, 80 Strand, London WC2R ORL, England
Penguin Group (USA) Inc., 375 Hudson Street, New York, New York 10014, USA
Penguin Group (Canada), 90 Eglinton Avenue East, Suite 700, Toronto, Ontario, Canada M4P 2Y3
(a division of Pearson Penguin Canada Inc.)
Penguin Ireland, 25 St Stephen's Green, Dublin 2, Ireland (a division of Penguin Books Ltd)
Penguin Group (Australia), 250 Camberwell Road, Camberwell, Victoria 3124, Australia
(a division of Pearson Australia Group Pty Ltd)
Penguin Books India Pvt Ltd, 11 Community Centre, Panchsheel Park, New Delhi – 110 017, India
Penguin Group (NZ), 67 Apollo Drive, Rosedale, North Shore 0632, New Zealand
(a division of Pearson New Zealand Ltd)
Penguin Books (South Africa) (Pty) Ltd, 24 Sturdee Avenue, Rosebank, Johannesburg 2196, South Africa

Penguin Books Ltd, Registered Offices: 80 Strand, London WC2R ORL, England

www.penguin.com

This selection first published 2009

1

Selection amd introduction copyright © Owen Sheers, 2009
BBC and the BBC logo are trademarks of the British Broadcasting Company
and are used under licence. BBC logo © BBC 1996
The television programme, *A Poet's Guide to Britain*, is copyright © Prospect, a DCD Media Company

The moral right of the copyright-holders has been asserted

The Acknowledgements on pages 327–33 constitute an extension of this copyright page

A CIP catalogue record for this book is available from the British Library

ISBN: 978-0-141-19202-4

www.greenpenguin.co.uk

Contents

Mountains and Moorland

Islands

Woods and Forests

Coast and Sea

Acknowledgements

The compilation of this anthology would not have been possible without the support and enthusiasm of David Smith and Lyndsi Barnes at the New York Public Library. I am indebted to them for their assistance in finding, copying and organizing a huge amount of material in a short space of time.

I am also grateful to Fiona Morris for so energetically pursuing the idea of getting *A Poet's Guide to Britain* on to television, to Jacquie Hughes for getting on board and Janice Hadlow for setting us on our way. Once on the journey I couldn't have asked for better travelling companions than Rupert Edwards and Karen McCallion. I'd like to thank Alexis Kirschbaum at Penguin for allowing me to expand upon the ideas of that series and for giving the whole endeavour a permanent home in this book.

Of *Albion*'s glorious Isle the wonders whilst I write,
The sundry varying soils, the pleasures infinite,
(Where heat kills not the cold, nor cold expells the heat,
The calms too mildly small, nor winds too roughly great,
Nor night doth hinder day, nor day the night doth wrong,
The summer not too short, the winter not too long)
What help shall I invoke to aid my Muse the while?
    Thou *Genius* of the place (this most renownéd Isle)
Which livedst long before the all-earth-drowning Flood,
Whilst yet the world did swarm with her Giganticbrood,
Go thou before me still thy circling shores about,
And in this wand'ring maze help to conduct me out:
Direct my course so right, as with thy hand to show
Which way thy Forests range, which way thy Rivers flow;
Wise *Genius*, by thy help that so I may descry
How thy Fair Mountains stand, and how thy Valleys lie

Michael Drayton, from *Poly-Olbion*, 'The First Song'

Introduction

'A place that, like a mirror, makes you see.'
U. A. Fanthorpe

I

This book is a selection of poetry about the landscape of Great Britain. Each section opens with and takes its theme from one of the six poems I explored in the BBC Four television series of the same title. I have interpreted the word 'Britain' in a geographical sense, choosing poems about places in England, Scotland, Wales and the archipelagos scattered off their shores.

A television series might be considered an unusual genesis for a selection of landscape poetry. The two mediums share more narrative DNA than some would give them credit for, but they are, in the end, very different animals. Television's pulse is faster than poetry's. If poetry is an active medium, then television tends towards the passive. Where television is a medium of compromise, poetry is liberatingly, wonderfully uncompromising. Television's focus is broad, its intentions aimed at the catch-as-many-as-you-can audience, while a poem is, I believe, written first and foremost for that most intimate of relationships between the voice of the poet and the ear and inner eye of the individual reader.

In the case of this book, however, this selection marks more of a closing of a circle than a continuation of a television series. It's a circle that begins with landscape itself. I fell in love with the experience of landscape, with how the hills and coasts of South Wales could alter my thoughts and feelings, long before I fell for poetry. It would be in poems, though, many of them included in this book, that I would find my experiences given words. My reading of those landscape poems eventually led to a television series which has, in turn, led me back to this book and the opportunity to bring together a selection of poems of place, to have them speak not just to a reader, but also to each other.

II

I say this is a book of *poetry about the landscape* of Great Britain, but of course landscape isn't all these poems are about. Their voices might be found in the varied topographies of the island of Britain, and in doing so these places are indeed described for us, painted with the poet's eye. But like any good poetry these poems also use the voices found in their subjects and settings to speak about other things, and to take us to other places. Primarily, they use them to speak about us – the people who live in, look at and remember the places of Britain which have, in turn, remembered us; as individuals, as communities, as history.

That poems of landscape are also poems about us shouldn't be surprising. After all, without us, landscape would not exist. There would be nature, but no landscape. Landscape is what happens to nature when we turn up; when her hills, forests and seas are passed through the prism of our imaginations to be refracted again as a painting, a view, a memory. It is our perception that brings landscape into being.

III

It's this human investment in landscape, this mutually dependent relationship, which has, over the centuries, provided such a rich seam for poets and poetry. The intention of a poem is often to make the abstract world of thought and feeling concrete; to use condensed and heightened language to talk about our inner and shared emotional and intellectual lives in terms of the physical world of things. Our landscapes, holding so much of us and our ancestors as they do, are physical places that come ready-sown with the associations, metaphors and memories upon which a poem feeds. They are laid out around us, made by us, waiting for the poet to mine them and so illuminate that which we thought we already knew, and make us see that which we thought we'd already seen.

This 'knowing' is another inherent quality of landscape. It is, to a certain extent, a shared and universal entity, in some cases across countries, languages, centuries and cultures. Step into a wood in Britain, in Romania, in America; stand beside the sea in Cornwall, by the Pacific, in Brazil, and the same essentials of the experience, especially the effects of that place upon our internal weather, will be known to a person in all those countries. And yet, within that shared experience, there will also be specific tones and notes of colour, lent to each by local climate, history and literature.

This element of a landscape, the simple fact that there is more than one way of 'knowing' a place, offers fertile territory for both the poet and the reader. In his essay *The Sense of Place*, Seamus Heaney identifies two dominant complimentary and yet anti-pathetic ways of knowing a landscape: 'One is lived, illiterate and unconscious, the other learned, literate and conscious. In the literary sensibility, both are likely to co-exist in a conscious and unconscious tension.'

It's this tension, between the unconscious and conscious knowing of a place, that has produced many of the poems in this anthology, and which lends the best of them a double-sensation of recollection and illumination; of being presented with something familiar and yet also shown something new. 'The waving of the boughs in the storm', Emerson writes, 'is new to me and old. It takes me by surprise, and yet is not unknown.' For me, this describes exactly what the best landscape poetry can offer; an experience 'new to me and old', one which expands my existing knowledge of a place to change the way I will see and experience that place, or a type of place, for ever. The poem which opens the 'Woods and Forests' section, Louis MacNeice's 'Woods', is an example of this. Ever since reading it I have been unable to step into a wood without these lines from the poem echoing in my ear,

> . . . a dark
> But gentle ambush . . .
> . . .a kingdom free from time and sky,
> Caterpillar webs on the forehead, danger under the feet,
> And the mind adrift in a floating and rustling ark

IV

Your guides in this book are the poems that I believe do just this – refresh and deepen our experience of the places around us and, through them, of ourselves. The selection of the poems is mine, but it's the poems themselves, and the poets who wrote them, who will take you on a journey. Not just through Britain's cities, towns, woods, villages and islands, but also through her history and, at times, deeper again, into the multiple personalities of her psyche. Taken together I hope these poets and their poems will create a poetic map of the island of Britain, one that charts her darkest corners as well as her brightest summits, that explores her inner as well as her outer territories.

V

Although the television series was a result, rather than the root, of my interest in the poems in this anthology, it has had a significant influence over their organization. I've already mentioned how this book borrows the foundation architecture of the series, dividing the poems into six sections, each of which explores six types of British landscape. But it's in the more intimate architecture within those sections that the thesis of the series really exerts a shaping pressure.

The idea driving *A Poet's Guide to Britain* was that such a rich variety of landscapes packed on to an island as small as Britain has led, over the years, to a particularly vital conversation between Britain's poets and her places. The other idea in each programme was to use the poem we were looking at as a door into other poems and other places, to follow threads of association to contemporary poets who shared some kind of territory, either geographical or thematic, with the original poem or poet.

It's these ideas of conversation and association that define the ordering principle for this anthology. In each section every poem, in some way, speaks to the next and, in some way, listens to the one before. They are links in a chain, sometimes joined by geography, at other times by how they respond to the type of landscape in question. The first line of one poem might answer the last line of another; one poem might question or contradict another; two poets divided by centuries might be joined by a common revelation. Whatever the connection between the poems, there is one, creating, I hope, an echo-chamber of call and response, of speaking and listening, which comes together to form a deepening excavation of what that particular landscape means for, and says about, Britain and the British.

It's for this reason that I would recommend reading each section in order, starting with the first poem and finishing with the last. If you do that it's my hope that you'll be taken on several kinds of journey at once. You'll travel through Britain, but you'll also travel through the conversation I described and, via that conversation, through the different facets and qualities of the landscape at its heart.

VI

I compiled this selection of poems in the New York Public Library in Manhattan, over 3,000 miles away from their subject. Each morning I would return to my desk in the Allen Room and, through the poems in the books piled on it, travel back to Britain. Reading those poems, so far away from the places they described, I felt as if I were putting my ear to an atlas of the country. As the poems evoked and remembered its history, languages, accents and top-ographies, I felt as if I were listening to the voice of the island itself, gradually gaining volume, poem by poem. When I left the library at the end of the day, that voice of Britain would still be loud in my ear, woven between the hysterical fire trucks and honking cabs of Fifth Avenue at rush hour.

As you read these poems, I would encourage you to listen too, particularly to how the journeys within each section are mapped by both a variety and a consistency of poetic response. What I mean by that is how each poem reveals something new about a landscape while also often remembering something in its experi-ence that is shared by other poems across the centuries, genders and locations. Again and again woods and trees are addressed directly or given voice themselves; cities offer up, from within their maelstroms of humanity, glimpses of the best and the worst of the individual; the ocean crashing at our shores constantly brings poets across ages and cultures to liminal inner places of challenge and reflection, while our villages and towns are repeatedly left and returned to over the years, vessels of childhood memory marking the divides between who we were and who we are.

VII

By organizing these poems in such an associative manner this selection is free of historical divisions. A poem of the twenty-first century might follow one from the eighteenth, which in turn follows a poem from the tenth. I hope this historical hop-scotching will emphasize rather than dilute the ongoing nature of the conversations between poets and the British landscape, and between the poets themselves.

When E. M. Forster gathers the novelists of the ages together in his *Aspects of the Novel*, he does so around one massive table. In this anthology, however, I'd like to think of the poets all strolling around one large garden, sometimes seeing each other in the distance, sometimes passing by close enough to pick up snatches of conversation, sometimes stopping to talk intimately one to one, sometimes taking up a position on a bench to address a small crowd. Although each of them occupies his or her own particular space, and is possessed of an individual idiolect and local perception, none of them are writing about landscape without an awareness of those others who are writing around them, or who have written about it before them.

VIII

I hope this shared conversation lends this selection a timeless quality – the nature of our relationships with woods, mountains, cities and seas, echoing through the centuries and generations. I can't help feeling, however, that a selection of landscape poetry, of poems about how we are our landscape, and it is us, is also particularly timely right now.

Climate change and its consequences presents one of the greatest contemporary threats to human civilization on the planet. It is a problem that has grown from both our technical brilliance and our talent for divorcing cause and consequence. Despite being better equipped than ever before, it is also the result of our failure to read and listen to the effect of our actions upon the landscape around us.

What can poems and poetry do about this? In the grand scheme of things, probably very little. They can, though, remind us that what is under threat is not just the natural world, but everything of us that it holds. That we don't just depend physically on the landscapes around us but also spiritually and emotionally. Poets of the landscape are gamekeepers of our cultural and communal memories, the finders and the keepers of landscape's metaphoric qualities. They are, too, seers, who in deepening our understanding of the landscape around us, also deepen our understanding of ourselves. Their poems about our environments are reminders that unless we embrace a more sustainable culture, then the shared experiences of generations, and therefore our knowledge of ourselves, will be drastically culled. To quote Gerard Manley Hopkins on the felling of his poplars, 'After-comers cannot guess the beauty been.'

IX

The reason I read poetry is for its equation of 'less is more', for the way in which, by playing 'the rhythms of dramatic speech on the grid of meter' (Robert Frost) it can use a few words over a short space of page to transport us a great emotional and intellectual distance. It is, I believe, often the best way we have of saying many things at once.

In keeping with this belief it seems only right I finish this introduction with the poem that introduced each programme in the television series. I hope it goes some way towards conveying in fewer words everything I've tried to say with more in the previous pages.

> There are places that speak,
> telling the stories of us and them.
>
> A village asleep, loaded with dream,
> an ocean, flicking its pages over the sand.
>
> Eventually we reply, a conversation
> of place and page over time,
>
> inscribing the map so that each,
> in turn, might hold the line.

London and Cities

WILLIAM WORDSWORTH

Composed Upon Westminster Bridge
Sept. 3, 1802

Earth has not any thing to shew more fair:
Dull would he be of soul who could pass by
A sight so touching in its majesty:
This City now doth like a garment wear
The beauty of the morning; silent, bare,
Ships, towers, domes, theatres, and temples lie
Open unto the fields, and to the sky;
All bright and glittering in the smokeless air.
Never did sun more beautifully steep
In his first splendor valley, rock, or hill;
Ne'er saw I, never felt, a calm so deep!
The river glideth at his own sweet will:
Dear God! the very houses seem asleep;
And all that mighty heart is lying still!

ALICE OSWALD

Another Westminster Bridge

go and glimpse the lovely inattentive water
discarding the gaze of many a bored street walker

where the weather trespasses into strip-lit offices
through tiny windows into tiny thoughts and authorities

and the soft beseeching tapping of typewriters

take hold of a breath-width instant, stare
at water which is already elsewhere
in a scrapwork of flashes and glittery flutters
and regular waves of apparently motionless motion

under the teetering structures of administration

where a million shut-away eyes glance once
restlessly at the river's ruts and glints

count five, then wander swiftly
away over the stone wing-bone of the city

T. S. ELIOT

from *The Wasteland*,
I. The Burial of the Dead

Unreal City,
Under the brown fog of a winter dawn,
A crowd flowed over London Bridge, so many,
I had not thought death had undone so many.
Sighs, short and infrequent, were exhaled,
And each man fixed his eyes before his feet.
Flowed up the hill and down King William Street,
To where Saint Mary Woolnoth kept the hours
With a dead sound on the final stroke of nine.
There I saw one I knew, and stopped him, crying: 'Stetson!
'You who were with me in the ships at Mylae!
'That corpse you planted last year in your garden,
'Has it begun to sprout? Will it bloom this year?
'Or has the sudden frost disturbed its bed?
'O keep the Dog far hence, that's friend to men,
'Or with his nails he'll dig it up again!
'You! hypocrite lecteur!—mon semblable,—mon frère!'

ANONYMOUS (C. 1726)

London Bridge

London Bridge is broken down,
  Broken down, broken down,
London Bridge is broken down,
  My fair lady.

Build it up with wood and clay,
  Wood and clay, wood and clay,
Build it up with wood and clay,
  My fair lady.

Wood and clay will wash away,
  Wash away, wash away,
Wood and clay will wash away,
  My fair lady.

Build it up with bricks and mortar,
  Bricks and mortar, bricks and mortar,
Build it up with bricks and mortar,
  My fair lady.

Bricks and mortar will not stay,
  Will not stay, will not stay,
Bricks and mortar will not stay,
  My fair lady.

Build it up with iron and steel,
  Iron and steel, iron and steel,
Build it up with iron and steel,
  My fair lady.

Iron and steel will bend and bow,
  Bend and bow, bend and bow,
Iron and steel will bend and bow,
  My fair lady.

Build it up with silver and gold,
  Silver and gold, silver and gold,
Build it up with silver and gold,
  My fair lady.

Silver and gold will be stolen away,
  Stolen away, stolen away,
Silver and gold will be stolen away,
  My fair lady.

Set a man to watch all night,
  Watch all night, watch all night,
Set a man to watch all night,
  My fair lady.

Suppose the man should fall asleep,
  Fall asleep, fall asleep,
Suppose the man should fall asleep?
  My fair lady.

Give him a pipe to smoke all night,
  Smoke all night, smoke all night,
Give him a pipe to smoke all night,
  My fair lady.

MARY ROBINSON

London's Summer Morning

Who has not waked to list the busy sounds
Of summer's morning, in the sultry smoke
Of noisy London? On the pavement hot
The sooty chimney-boy, with dingy face
And tatter'd covering, shrilly bawls his trade,
Rousing the sleepy housemaid. At the door
The milk-pail rattles, and the tinkling bell
Proclaims the dustman's office; while the street
Is lost in clouds impervious. Now begins
The din of hackney-coaches, waggons, carts;
While tinmen's shops, and noisy trunk-makers,
Knife-grinders, coopers, squeaking cork-cutters,
Fruit barrows, and the hunger-giving cries
Of vegetable venders, fill the air.
Now every shop displays its varied trade,
And the fresh-sprinkled pavement cools the feet
Of early walkers. At the private door
The ruddy housemaid twirls the busy mop,
Annoying the smart 'prentice, or neat girl,
Tripping with band-box lightly. Now the sun
Darts burning splendour on the glittering pane,
Save where the canvas awning throws a shade
On the day merchandize. Now, spruce and trim,
In shops (where beauty smiles with industry),
Sits the smart damsel; while the passenger
Peeps through the window, watching every charm.
Now pastry dainties catch the eye minute
Of humming insects, while the limy snare
Waits to enthral them. Now the lamp-lighter
Mounts the tall ladder, nimbly venturous,
To trim the half-fill'd lamp; while at his feet
The pot-boy yells discordant! All along
The sultry pavement, the old-clothes man cries

In tone monotonous, the side-long views
The area for his traffic: now the bag
Is slily open'd, and the half-worn suit
(Sometimes the pilfer'd treasure of the base
Domestic spoiler), for one half its worth,
Sinks in the green abyss. The porter now
Bears his huge load along the burning way;
And the poor poet wakes from busy dreams,
To paint the summer morning.

To the City of London

London, thou art of townes A *per se.*
  Soveraign of cities, semeliest in sight,
Of high renoun, riches, and royaltie;
  Of lordis, barons, and many goodly knyght;
  Of most delectable lusty ladies bright;
Of famous prelatis in habitis clericall;
  Of merchauntis full of substaunce and myght:
London, thou art the flour of Cities all.

Gladdith anon, thou lusty Troy Novaunt,
  Citie that some tyme cleped was New Troy,
In all the erth, imperiall as thou stant,
  Pryncesse of townes, of pleasure, and of joy,
  A richer restith under no Christen roy;
For manly power, with craftis naturall,
  Fourmeth none fairer sith the flode of Noy:
London, thou art the flour of Cities all.

Gemme of all joy, jasper of jocunditie,
  Most myghty carbuncle of vertue and valour;
Strong Troy in vigour and in strenuitie;
  Of royall cities rose and geraflour;
  Empresse of townes, exalt in honour;
In beawtie beryng the crone imperiall;
  Swete paradise precelling in pleasure:
London, thou art the flour of Cities all.

Above all ryvers thy Ryver hath renowne,
  Whose beryall stremys, pleasaunt and preclare,
Under thy lusty wallys renneth down,
  Where many a swanne doth swymme with wyngis fare;

Where many a barge doth saile, and row with are,
Where many a ship doth rest with toppe-royall.
   O! towne of townes, patrone and not-compare:
London, thou art the flour of Cities all.

Upon thy lusty Brigge of pylers white
   Been merchauntis full royall to behold;
Upon thy sretis goth many a semely knyght
   In velvet gownes and cheynes of fyne gold.
   By Julyus Cesar thy Tour founded of old
May be the hous of Mars victoryall,
   Whos artillary with tonge may not be told:
London, thou art the flour of Cities all.

Strong by thy wallis that about the standis;
   Wise by the people that within the dwellis;
Fresh is thy ryver with his lusty strandis;
   Blith be thy chirches, wele sownyng be thy bellis;
   Riche be thy merchauntis in substaunce that excellis;
Fair be thy wives, right lovesom, white and small;
   Clere be thy virgyns, lusty under kellis:
London, thou art the flour of Cities all.

Thy famous Maire, by pryncely governaunce,
   With swerd of justice the rulith prudently.
No Lord of Parys, Venyce, or Floraunce
   In dignytie or honoure goeth to hym nye.
   He is exampler, loode-ster, and guye;
Principall patrone and roose orygynalle,
   Above all Maires as maister moost worthy:
London, thou art the flour of Cities all.

WALTER SCOTT

'Edinburgh'
from *Marmion*

Caledonia's Queen is changed,
Since on her dusky summit ranged,
Within its steepy limits pent,
By bulwark, line, and battlement,
And flanking towers, and laky flood,
Guarded and garrison'd she stood,
Denying entrance or resort,
Save at each tall embattled port;
Above whose arch, suspended, hung
Portcullis spiked with iron prong.
That long is gone, – but not so long,
Since, early closed, and opening late,
Jealous revolved the studded gate,
Whose task, from eve to morning tide,
A wicket churlishly supplied.
Stern then, and steel-girt was thy brow,
Dunedin! O, how alter'd now,
When safe amid thy mountain court
Thou sitt'st, like empress at her sport,
And liberal, unconfined, and free,
Flinging thy white arms to the sea,
For thy dark cloud, with umber'd lower,
That hung o'er cliff, and lake, and tower,
Thou gleam'st against the western ray
Ten thousand lines of brighter day.

ALEXANDER SMITH

Glasgow

Sing, Poet, 'tis a merry world;
That cottage smoke is rolled and curled
   In sport, that every moss
Is happy, every inch of soil; –
Before *me* runs a road of toil
   With my grave cut across.
Sing, trailing showers and breezy downs –
I know the tragic hearts of towns.

City! I am true son of thine;
Ne'er dwelt I where great mornings shine
   Around the bleating pens;
Ne'er by the rivulets I strayed,
And ne'er upon my childhood weighed
   The silence of the glens.
Instead of shores where ocean beats,
I hear the ebb and flow of streets.

Black Labour draws his weary waves,
Into their secret-moaning caves;
   But with the morning light,
That sea again will overflow
With a long weary sound of woe,
   Again to faint in night.
Wave am I in that sea of woes,
Which, night and morning, ebbs and flows.

I dwelt within a gloomy court,
Wherein did never sunbeam sport;
  Yet there my heart was stirr'd.
My very blood did dance and thrill,
When on my narrow window-sill,
  Spring lighted like a bird.
Poor flowers – I watched them pine for weeks,
With leaves as pale as human cheeks.

Afar, one summer, I was borne;
Through golden vapours of the morn,
  I heard the hills of sheep:
I trod with a wild ecstasy
The bright fringe of the living sea:
  And on a ruined keep
I sat, and watched an endless plain
Blacken beneath the gloom of rain.

O fair the lightly sprinkled waste,
O'er which a laughing shower has raced!
  O fair the April shoots!
O fair the woods on summer days,
While a blue hyacinthine haze
  Is dreaming round the roots!
In thee, O City! I discern
Another beauty, sad and stern.

Draw thy fierce streams of blinding ore,
Smite on a thousand anvils, roar
  Down to the harbour-bars;
Smoulder in smoky sunsets, flare
On rainy nights, when street and square
  Lie empty to the stars.
From terrace proud to alley base
I know thee as my mother's face.

When sunset bathes thee in his gold,
In wreaths of bronze thy sides are rolled,
    Thy smoke is dusky fire;
And, from the glory round thee poured,
A sunbeam like an angel's sword
    Shivers upon a spire.
Thus have I watched thee, Terror! Dream!
While the blue Night crept up the stream.

The wild Train plunges in the hills,
He shrieks across the midnight rills;
    Streams through the shifting glare,
The roar and flap of foundry fires,
That shake with light the sleeping shires;
    And on the moorlands bare,
He sees afar a crown of light
Hang o'er thee in the hollow night.

At midnight, when thy suburbs lie
As silent as a noonday sky,
    When larks with heat are mute,
I love to linger on thy bridge.
All lonely as a mountain ridge.
    Disturbed but by my foot;
While the black lazy stream beneath,
Steals from its far-off wilds of heath.

And through thy heart, as through a dream,
Flows on that black disdainful stream;
    All scornfully it flows,
Between the huddled gloom of masts,
Silent as pines unvexed by blasts –
    'Tween lamps in streaming rows.
O wondrous sight! O stream of dread!
O long dark river of the dead!

Afar, the banner of the year
Unfurls: but dimly prisoned here,
    Tis only when I greet
A dropt rose lying in my way,
A butterfly that flutters gay
    Athwart the noisy street,
I know the happy Summer smiles
Around thy suburbs, miles on miles.

'T were neither pæan now, nor dirge,
The flash and thunder of the surge
    On flat sands wide and bare;
No haunting joy or anguish dwells
In the green light of sunny dells,
    Or in the starry air.
Alike to me the desert flower,
The rainbow laughing o'er the shower.

While o'er thy walls the darkness sails,
I lean against the churchyard rails;
    Up in the midnight towers
The belfried spire, the street is dead,
I hear in silence overhead
    The clang of iron hours:
It moves me not – I know her tomb
Is yonder in the shapeless gloom.

All raptures of this mortal breath,
Solemnities of life and death,
    Dwell in thy noise alone:
Of me thou hast become a part –
Some kindred with my human heart
    Lives in thy streets of stone;
For we have been familiar more
Than galley-slave and weary oar.

The beech is dipped in wine; the shower
Is burnished; on the swinging flower
   The latest bee doth sit.
The low sun stares through dust of gold,
And o'er the darkening heath and wold
   The large ghost-moth doth flit.
In every orchard Autumn stands,
With apples in his golden hands.

But all these sights and sounds are strange;
Then wherefore from thee should I range?
   Thou hast my kith and kin:
My childhood, youth, and manhood brave;
Thou hast that unforgotten grave
   Within thy central din.
   A sacredness of love and death
Dwells in thy noise and smoky breath.

EDWIN MORGAN

from *Glasgow Sonnets*

I

A mean wind wanders through the backcourt trash.
Hackles on puddles rise, old mattresses
puff briefly and subside. Play-fortresses
of brick and bric-a-brac spill out some ash.
Four storeys have no windows left to smash,
but in the fifth a chipped sill buttresses
mother and daughter the last mistresses
of that black block condemned to stand, not crash.
Around them the cracks deepen, the rats crawl.
The kettle whimpers on a crazy hob.
Roses of mould grow from ceiling to wall.
The man lies late since he has lost his job,
smokes on one elbow, letting his coughs fall
thinly into an air too poor to rob.

IV

Down by the brickworks you get warm at least.
Surely soup-kitchens have gone out? It's not
the Thirties now. Hugh MacDiarmid forgot
in 'Glasgow 1960' that the feast
of reason and the flow of soul have ceased
to matter to the long unfinished plot
of heating frozen hands. We never got
an abstruse song that charmed the raging beast.
So you have nothing to lose but your chains,
dear Seventies. Dalmarnock, Maryhill,
Blackhill and Govan, better sticks and stanes
should break your banes, for poets' words are ill
to hurt ye. On the wrecker's ball the rains
of greeting cities drop and drink their fill.

VI

The North Sea oil-strike tilts east Scotland up,
and the great sick Clyde shivers in its bed.
But elegists can't hang themselves on fled-
from trees or poison a recycled cup –
If only a less faint, shaky sunup
glimmered through the skeletal shop and shed
and men washed round the piers like gold and spread
golder in soul than Mitsubishi or Krupp –
The images are ageless but the thing
is now. Without my images the men
ration their cigarettes, their children cling
to broken toys, their women wonder when
the doors will bang on laughter and a wing
over the firth be simply joy again.

SEAN O'BRIEN

Autumn Begins at St James's Park, Newcastle
Homage to James Wright

Under the arc, the Toon Army tsunami,
Under three o'clock's great cry on Gallowgate,
Remember the lost world, politics: cages flying
Up from the pit and disgorging their democrats,
Helmeted, in blackface, by the thousand,
Like the sappers of the Somme.

A seated army of convicts
Will be thundering WOR BALL
At faintheart southern referees all winter.

At freezing dusk the bloodbucket bars are stowed out.
Mortgaged to football, the underclass raises
A glass to the ghost of itself
In a world without women or work.

ANNE STEVENSON

17.14 *Out of Newcastle*

Mostly feeling pity,
but sometimes fury
in the press of the crowd,

I scan it for an eye
to talk to, not aloud
but stealthily, quickly,

as one shade
might sign to another
in the queue for Avernus.

Here, we agree,
is where the incurious
or damned unlucky

live on in body
when the spirit dies
On such a train,

in some murky
siding of a poet's brain,
Limbo was devised

where there's no agony
and no joy, either,
just fleshy emptiness

sweating out the space between
weary I-am-ness
and the unloved pack.

As face retreats from face
to coverts of soft porn,
football, lust in paperback,

the old, waste, token city
(church and castle)
vanishes along the line,

resurrecting in a chain of
rainbows – steel riveted
ribcage for the breathing Tyne.

Put down your book.
Lift up your eyes.
The river's awake and at work

in its leaping bridges.
Electric confetti
zig and zag along its pulse,

celebrating our immense
human smallness
with a carnival.

'Don't rot inside your body,
build your soul.'
Could be its theme song.

We rattle over the rail bridge,
beating along.
Dum diddy, dum diddy . . .

There are too many of us.
Still, some undeniable voltage
wants to connect us.

DOUGLAS DUNN

A Removal from Terry Street

On a squeaking cart, they push the usual stuff,
A mattress, bed ends, cups, carpets, chairs,
Four paperback westerns. Two whistling youths
In surplus U.S. Army battle-jackets
Remove their sister's goods. Her husband
Follows, carrying on his shoulders the son
Whose mischief we are glad to see removed,
And pushing, of all things, a lawnmower.
There is no grass in Terry Street. The worms
Come up cracks in concrete yards in moonlight.
That man, I wish him well. I wish him grass.

DOUGLAS DUNN

On Roofs of Terry Street

Television aerials, Chinese characters
In the lower sky, wave gently in the smoke.

Nest-building sparrows peck at moss,
Urban flora and fauna, soft, unscrupulous.

Rain drying on the slates shines sometimes.
A builder is repairing someone's leaking roof.

He kneels upright to rest his back.
His trowel catches the light and becomes precious.

SIMON ARMITAGE

A Vision

The future was a beautiful place, once.
Remember the full-blown balsa-wood town
on public display in the Civic Hall?
The ring-bound sketches, artists' impressions,

blueprints of smoked glass and tubular steel,
board-game suburbs, modes of transportation
like fairground rides or executive toys.
Cities like *dreams*, cantilevered by light.

And people like us at the bottle bank
next to the cycle path, or dog-walking
over tended strips of fuzzy-felt grass,
or model drivers, motoring home in

electric cars. Or after the late show –
strolling the boulevard. They were the plans,
all underwritten in the neat left-hand
of architects – a true, legible script.

I pulled that future out of the north wind
at the landfill site, stamped with today's date,
riding the air with other such futures,
all unlived in and now fully extinct.

from *v*.

'My father still reads the dictionary every day. He says your
life depends on your power to master words.'
Arthur Scargill, *Sunday Times*, 10 Jan. 1982

Next millennium you'll have to search quite hard
to find my slab behind the family dead,
butcher, publican, and baker, now me, bard
adding poetry to their beef, beer and bread.

With Byron three graves on I'll not go short
of company, and Wordsworth's opposite.
That's two peers already, of a sort,
and we'll all be thrown together if the pit,

whose galleries once ran beneath this plot,
causes the distinguished dead to drop
into the rabblement of bone and rot,
shored slack, crushed shale, smashed prop.

Wordsworth built church organs, Byron tanned
luggage cowhide in the age of steam,
and knew their place of rest before the land
caves in on the lowest worked-out seam.

This graveyard on the brink of Beeston Hill's
the place I may well rest if there's a spot
under the rose roots and the daffodils
by which dad dignified the family plot.

If buried ashes saw then I'd survey
the places I learned Latin, and learned Greek,
and left, the ground where Leeds United play
but disappoint their fans week after week,

which makes them lose their sense of self-esteem
and taking a short cut home through these graves here
they reassert the glory of their team
by spraying words on tombstones, pissed on beer.

This graveyard stands above a worked-out pit.
Subsidence makes the obelisks all list.
One leaning left's marked FUCK, one right's marked SHIT
sprayed by some peeved supporter who was pissed.

Far-sighted for his family's future dead,
but for his wife, this banker's still alone
on his long obelisk, and doomed to head
a blackened dynasty of unclaimed stone,

now graffitied with a crude four-letter word.
His children and grand-children went away
and never came back home to be interred,
so left a lot of space for skins to spray.

The language of this graveyard ranges from
a bit of Latin for a former Mayor
or those who laid their lives down at the Somme,
the hymnal fragments and the gilded prayer,

how people 'fell asleep in the Good Lord',
brief chisellable bits from the good book
and rhymes whatever length they could afford,
to CUNT, PISS, SHIT and (mostly) FUCK!

Or, more expansively, there's LEEDS v.
the opponent of last week, this week, or next,
and a repertoire of blunt four-letter curses
on the team or race that makes the sprayer vexed.

Then, pushed for time, or fleeing some observer,
dodging between tall family vaults and trees
like his team's best ever winger, dribbler, swerver,
fills every space he finds with versus Vs.

Vs sprayed on the run at such a lick,
the sprayer master of his flourished tool,
get short-armed on the left like that red tick
they never marked his work much with at school.

Half this skinhead's age but with approval
I helped whitewash a V on a brick wall.
No one clamoured in the press for its removal
or thought the sign, in wartime, rude at all.

These Vs are all the versuses of life
from LEEDS v. DERBY, Black/White
and (as I've known to my cost) man v. wife,
Communist v. Fascist, Left v. Right,

class v. class as bitter as before,
the unending violence of US and THEM,
personified in 1984
by Coal Board MacGregor and the NUM,

Hindu/Sikh, soul/body, heart v. mind,
East/West, male/female, and the ground
these fixtures are fought out on 's Man, resigned
to hope from his future what his past never found.

The prospects for the present aren't too grand
when a swastika with NF (National Front) 's
sprayed on a grave, to which another hand
has added, in a reddish colour, CUNTS.

Which is, I grant, the word that springs to mind,
when going to clear the weeds and rubbish thrown
on the family plot by football fans, I find
UNITED graffitied on my parents' stone.

How many British graveyards now this May
are strewn with rubbish and choked up with weeds
since families and friends have gone away
for work or fuller lives, like me from Leeds?

When I first came here 40 years ago
with my dad to 'see my grandma' I was 7.
I helped dad with the flowers. He let me know
she'd gone to join my grandad up in Heaven.

My dad who came each week to bring fresh flowers
came home with clay stains on his trouser knees.
Since my parents' deaths I've spent 2 hours
made up of odd 10 minutes such as these.

Flying visits once or twice a year,
and though I'm horrified just who's to blame
that I find instead of flowers cans of beer
and more than one grave sprayed with some skin's name?

Where there were flower urns and troughs of water
and mesh receptacles for withered flowers
are the HARP tins of some skinhead Leeds supporter.
It isn't all his fault though. Much is ours.

5 kids, with one in goal, play 2-a-side.
When the ball bangs on the hawthorn that's one post
and petals fall they hum *Here Comes the Bride*
though not so loud they'd want to rouse a ghost.

They boot the ball on purpose at the trunk
and make the tree shed showers of shrivelled may.
I look at this word graffitied by some drunk
and I'm in half a mind to let it stay.

(Though honesty demands that I say *if*
I'd wanted to take the necessary pains
to scrub the skin's inscription off
I only had an hour between trains.

So the feelings that I had as I stood gazing
and the significance I saw could be a sham,
mere excuses for not patiently erasing
the word sprayed on the grave of dad and mam.)

This pen's all I have of magic wand.
I know this world's so torn but want no other
except for dad who'd hoped from 'the beyond'
a better life than this one, *with* my mother.

Though I don't believe in afterlife at all
and know it's cheating it's hard *not* to make
a sort of furtive prayer from this skin's scrawl,
his UNITED mean 'in Heaven' for their sake,

an accident of meaning to redeem
an act intended as mere desecration
and make the thoughtless spraying of his team
apply to higher things, and to the nation.

PAUL FARLEY

Liverpool Disappears for a Billionth
of a Second

Shorter than the blink inside a blink
the National Grid will sometimes make, when you'll
turn to a room and say: *Was that just me?*

People sitting down for dinner don't feel
their chairs taken away/put back again
much faster than that trick with tablecloths.

A train entering the Olive Mount cutting
shudders, but not a single passenger
complains when it pulls in almost on time.

The birds feel it, though, and if you see
starlings in shoal, seagulls abandoning
cathedral ledges, or a mob of pigeons

lifting from a square as at gunfire,
be warned, it may be happening, but then
those sensitive to bat-squeak in the backs

of necks, who claim to hear the distant roar
of comets on the turn – these may well smile
at a world restored, in one piece; though each place

where mineral Liverpool goes wouldn't believe
what hit it: all that sandstone out to sea
or meshed into the quarters of Cologne.

I've felt it a few times when I've gone home,
if anything, more often now I'm old,
and the gaps between get shorter all the time.

CAROL ANN DUFFY

North-West

However it is we return to the water's edge
where the ferry grieves down by the Pier Head,
we do what we always did and get on board.
The city drifts out of reach. A huge silvery bird,
a kiss on the lip of the wind, follows our ship.
This is where we were young, the place no map
or heritage guide can reveal. Only an X on a wave
marks the spot, the flowers of litter, a grave
for our ruined loves, unborn children, ghosts.
We look back at the skyline wondering what we lost
in the hidden streets, in the rented rooms,
no more than punters now in a tourist boom.
Above our heads the gulls cry *yeah yeah yeah*.
Frets of light on the river. Tearful air.

ADAM O'RIORDAN

Manchester

Queen of the cotton cities,
nightly I begin to piece you back into existence:

the frayed bridal train your chimneys lay
and the warped applause-track of Victorian rain.

You're the blackened lung whose depths I plumb,
the million windows and the smoke-occluded sun.

A girl steps from a door and her cotton flecked shawl
is the first snow on a turf-plot back in Mayo.

You're the globing of the world, a litany of little cities
cast and re-made in your image: *Osaka, Orizaba, Gabrovo.*

Your warehouses bloated by curious needs:
butter, shellfish, clog blocks, bleach.

Your urchins little merchants hawking Lucifers and besoms
to set a small flame guttering in a wet-brick basement:

in the straw and wood shavings a mother's lullabies
bear their freight of love and typhus.

In the small hours I remake you and remake you,
until you grow faint as a footfall on a fever ward

and I wake from my imagination's gas-lit parlour
and whatever I seek to have or hold or harbour

is pure curio – a wreath of feathers, seashells
or human hair, a taxidermist's diorama.

I Remember, I Remember

Coming up England by a different line
For once, early in the cold new year,
We stopped, and, watching men with number-plates
Sprint down the platform to familiar gates,
'Why, Coventry!' I exclaimed. 'I was born here.'

I leant far out, and squinnied for a sign
That this was still the town that had been 'mine'
So long, but found I wasn't even clear
Which side was which. From where those cycle-crates
Were standing, had we annually departed

For all those family hols? . . . A whistle went:
Things moved. I sat back, staring at my boots.
'Was that,' my friend smiled, 'where you "have your roots"?'
No, only where my childhood was unspent,
I wanted to retort, just where I started:

By now I've got the whole place clearly charted.
Our garden, first: where I did not invent
Blinding theologies of flowers and fruits,
And wasn't spoken to by an old hat.
And here we have that splendid family

I never ran to when I got depressed,
The boys all biceps and the girls all chest,
Their comic Ford, their farm where I could be
'Really myself'. I'll show you, come to that,
The bracken where I never trembling sat,

Determined to go through with it; where she
Lay back, and 'all became a burning mist'.
And, in those offices, my doggerel
Was not set up in blunt ten-point, nor read
By a distinguished cousin of the mayor,

Who didn't call and tell my father *There*
Before us, had we the gift to see ahead –
'You look as if you wished the place in Hell,'
My friend said, 'judging from your face.' 'Oh well,
I suppose it's not the place's fault,' I said.

'Nothing, like something, happens anywhere.'

LOUIS MACNEICE

Birmingham

Smoke from the train-gulf hid by hoardings blunders upward, the
    brakes of cars
Pipe as the policeman pivoting round raises his flat hand, bars
With his figure of a monolith Pharaoh the queue of fidgety
    machines
(Chromium dogs on the bonnet, faces behind the triplex screens).
Behind him the streets run away between the proud glass of
    shops,
Cubical scent-bottles artificial legs arctic foxes and electric mops,
But beyond this centre the slumward vista thins like a diagram:
There, unvisited, are Vulcan's forges who doesn't care a tinker's
    damn.

Splayed outwards through the suburbs houses, houses for rest
Seducingly rigged by the builder, half-timbered houses with lips
    pressed
So tightly and eyes staring at the traffic through bleary haws
And only a six-inch grip of the racing earth in their concrete
    claws;
In these houses men as in a dream pursue the Platonic Forms
With wireless and cairn terriers and gadgets approximating to
    the fickle norms
And endeavour to find God and score one over the neighbour
By climbing tentatively upward on jerry-built beauty and sweated
    labour.

The lunch hour: the shops empty, shopgirls' faces relax
Diaphanous as green glass, empty as old almanacs
As incoherent with ticketed gewgaws tiered behind their heads
As the Burne-Jones windows in St Philip's broken by crawling
    leads;

Insipid colour, patches of emotion, Saturday thrills
(This theatre is sprayed with 'June') – the gutter take our old
    playbills,
Next week-end it is likely in the heart's funfair we shall pull
Strong enough on the handle to get back our money; or at any
    rate it is possible.

On shining lines the trams like vast sarcophagi move
Into the sky, plum after sunset, merging to duck's egg, barred
    with mauve
Zeppelin clouds, and Pentecost-like the cars' headlights bud
Out from sideroads and the traffic signals, crème-de-menthe or
    bull's blood,
Tell one to stop, the engine gently breathing, or to go on
To where like black pipes of organs in the frayed and fading zone
Of the West the factory chimneys on sullen sentry will all night
    wait
To call, in the harsh morning, sleep-stupid faces through the
    daily gate.

DANNIE ABSE

Return to Cardiff

'Hometown'; well, most admit an affection for a city:
grey, tangled streets I cycled on to school, my first cigarette
in the back lane, and, fool, my first botched love affair.
First everything. Faded torments; self-indulgent pity.

The journey to Cardiff seemed less a return than a raid
on mislaid identities. Of course the whole locus smaller:
the mile-wide Taff now a stream, the castle not as in some black,
gothic dream, but a decent sprawl, a joker's toy façade.

Unfocused voices in the wind, associations, clues,
odds and ends, fringes caught, as when, after the doctor quit,
a door opened and I glimpsed the white, enormous face
of my grandfather, suddenly aghast with certain news.

Unable to define anything I can hardly speak,
and still I love the place for what I wanted it to be
as much as for what it unashamedly is
now for me, a city of strangers, alien and bleak.

Unable to communicate I'm easily betrayed,
uneasily diverted by mere sense reflections
like those anchored waterscapes that wander, alter, in the Taff,
hour by hour, as light slants down a different shade.

Illusory, too, that lost dark playground after rain,
the noise of trams, gunshots in what they once called Tiger Bay.
Only real this smell of ripe, damp earth when the sun comes out,
a mixture of pungencies, half exquisite and half plain.

No sooner than I'd arrived the other Cardiff had gone,
smoke in the memory, these but tinned resemblances,
where the boy I was not and the man I am not
met, hesitated, left double footsteps, then walked on.

IDRIS DAVIES

Queen Street, Cardiff

When the crowds flow into Queen Street from the suburbs and
    the hills
And the music of the hour is the music of the tills,
I sometimes gaze and wonder at my fellows passing by,
Each one with dreams and passions, each one to toil and die.

And I almost hear the voices of a throng I never knew
That passed through this same Queen Street, and under skies as
    blue,
And they too had their laughter, their sorrow, in their day,
And they too went a journey with an unreturning way.

And other generations in distant years to be
Shall walk and crowd through Queen Street, in joy or misery,
And they shall laugh and grumble and love and hate and lust,
Their living flesh oblivious of our eternal dust.

But banish all such brooding, for May is in the air,
And Jack from Ystrad Mynach loves Jill from Aberdare,
And however Life shall use them, they shall talk in years to be
Of when they were young in Queen Street in the city by the sea.

W. H. AUDEN

Oxford

Nature invades: old rooks in each college garden
Still talk, like agile babies, the language of feeling,
By towers a river still runs coastward and will run,
    Stones in those towers are utterly
    Satisfied still with their weight.

Mineral and creature, so deeply in love with themselves
Their sin of accidie excludes all others,
Challenge our high-strung students with a careless beauty,
    Setting a single error
    Against their countless faults.

Outside, some factories, then a whole green county
Where a cigarette comforts the evil, a hymn the weak,
Where thousands fidget and poke and spend their money:
    Eros Paidagogos
    Weeps on his virginal bed.

And over this talkative city like any other
Weep the non-attached angels. Here too the knowledge of
    death
Is a consuming love, and the natural heart refuses
    A low unflattering voice
    That sleeps not till it find a hearing.

from *Don Juan*, Cantos 10, 11 and 13

... Juan now was borne,
Just as the day began to wane and darken,
  O'er the high hill which looks with pride or scorn
Towards the great city. Ye who have a spark in
  Your veins of Cockney spirit smile or mourn,
According as you take things well or ill.
Bold Britons, we are now on Shooter's Hill.

The sun went down, the smoke rose up, as from
  A half-unquenched volcano, o'er a space
Which well beseemed the 'devil's drawing room',
  As some have qualified that wondrous place.
But Juan felt, though not approaching home,
  As one who, though he were not of the race,
Revered the soil, of those true sons the mother,
Who butchered half the earth and bullied t'other.

A mighty mass of brick and smoke and shipping,
  Dirty and dusky, but as wide as eye
Could reach, with here and there a sail just skipping
  In sight, then lost amidst the forestry
Of masts, a wilderness of steeples peeping
  On tiptoe through their sea coal canopy,
A huge, dun cupola, like a foolscap crown
On a fool's head – and there is London town!

... Hail, Thamis, hail! Upon thy verge it is
That Juan's chariot, rolling like a drum
  In thunder, holds the way it can't well miss,
Through Kennington and all the other 'tons',
Which makes us wish ourselves in town at once;

Through groves, so called as being void of trees
   (Like *lucus* from no light); through prospects named
Mount Pleasant, as containing nought to please
   Nor much to climb; through little boxes framed
Of bricks, to let the dust in at your ease,
   With 'To be let' upon their doors proclaimed;
Through 'Rows' most modestly called 'Paradise',
Which Eve might quit without much sacrifice;

Through coaches, drays, choked turnpikes, and a whirl
   Of wheels, and roar of voices and confusion.
Here taverns wooing to a pint of 'purl';
   There mails fast flying off like a delusion;
There barber's blocks with periwigs in curl
   In windows; here the lamplighter's infusion
Slowly distilled into the glimmering glass
(For in those days we had not got to gas).

Through this and much and more is the approach
   Of travellers to mighty Babylon.
Whether they come by horse or chaise or coach,
   With slight exceptions, all the ways seem one.
I could say more, but do not choose to encroach
   Upon the guidebook's privilege. The sun
Had set some time, and night was on the ridge
Of twilight as the party crossed the bridge.

That's rather fine, the gentle sound of Thamis,
   Who vindicates a moment too his stream,
Though hardly heard through multifarious 'damme's'.
   The lamps of Westminster's more regular gleam,
The breadth of pavement, and yon shrine where Fame is
   A spectral resident, whose pallid beam
In shape of moonshine hovers o'er the pile,
Make this a sacred part of Albion's isle.

The Druid's groves are gone – so much the better.
   Stonehenge is not, but what the devil is it?
But Bedlam still exists with its sage fetter,
   That madmen may not bite you on a visit.
The Bench too seats or suits full many a debtor.
   The Mansion House too (though some people quiz it)
To me appears a stiff yet grand erection.
But then the Abbey's worth the whole collection.

Over the stones still rattling up Pall Mall
   Through crowds and carriages, but waxing thinner
As thundered knockers broke the long-sealed spell
   Of doors 'gainst duns, and to an early dinner
Admitted a small party as night fell,
   Don Juan, our young diplomatic sinner,
Pursued his path and drove past some hotels,
St James's Palace and St James's hells.

They reached the hotel. Forth streamed from the front door
   A tide of well-clad waiters, and around
The mob stood and as usual several score
   Of those pedestrian Paphians, who abound
In decent London when the daylight's o'er.
   Commodious but immoral, they are found
Useful, like Malthus, in promoting marriage.
But Juan now is stepping from his carriage

Into one of the sweetest of hotels,
   Especially for foreigners and mostly
For those whom favour or whom fortune swells
   And cannot find a bill's small items costly.
There many an envoy either dwelt or dwells
   (The den of many a diplomatic lost lie),
Until to some conspicuous square they pass
And blazon o'er the door their names in brass.

'Tis true I might have chosen Piccadilly,
　A place where peccadilloes are unknown,
But I have motives, whether wise or silly,
　For letting that pure sanctuary alone.
Therefore I name not square, street, place, until I
　Find one where nothing naughty can be shown,
A vestal shrine of innocence of heart.
Such are – but I have lost the London chart.

WILLIAM BLAKE

London

I wander through each chartered street,
Near where the chartered Thames does flow,
And mark in every face I meet,
Marks of weakness, marks of woe.

In every cry of every man,
In every infant's cry of fear,
In every voice, in every ban,
The mind-forged manacles I hear:

How the chimney-sweeper's cry
Every blackening church appals,
And the hapless soldier's sigh
Runs in blood down palace-walls.

But most, through midnight streets I hear
How the youthful harlot's curse
Blasts the new-born infant's tear,
And blights with plagues the marriage-hearse.

SAMUEL JOHNSON

from *London: A Poem in Imitation of the Third Satire of Juvenal*

Tho' grief and fondness in my breast rebel,
When injur'd THALES bids the town farewell,
Yet still my calmer thoughts his choice commend,
I praise the hermit, but regret the friend,
Resolved at length, from vice and LONDON far,
To breathe in distant fields a purer air,
And, fix'd on Cambria's solitary shore,
Give to St David one true Briton more.
   For who would leave, unbrib'd, Hibernia's land,
Or change the rocks of Scotland for the Strand?
There none are swept by sudden fate away,
But all whom hunger spares, with age decay:
Here malice, rapine, accident, conspire,
And now a rabble rages, now a fire;
Their ambush here relentless ruffians lay,
And here the fell attorney prowls for prey;
Here falling houses thunder on your head,
And here a female atheist talks you dead.

. . . By numbers here from shame or censure free,
All crimes are safe, but hated poverty.
This, only this, the rigid law pursues,
This, only this, provokes the snarling muse.
The sober trader at a tatter'd cloak,
Wakes from his dream, and labours for a joke;
With brisker air the silken courtiers gaze,
And turn the varied taunt a thousand ways.
Of all the griefs that harrass the distress'd,
Sure the most bitter is a scornful jest;
Fate never wounds more deep the gen'rous heart,
Than when a blockhead's insult points the dart.

Has heaven reserv'd, in pity to the poor,
No pathless waste, or undiscover'd shore;
No secret island in the boundless main?
No peaceful desart yet unclaim'd by SPAIN?
Quick let us rise, the happy seats explore,
And bear oppression's insolence no more.
This mournful truth is ev'ry where confess'd,
SLOW RISES WORTH, BY POVERTY DEPRESS'D:
But here more slow, where all are slaves to gold,
Where looks are merchandise, and smiles are sold;
Where won by bribes, by flatteries implor'd,
The groom retails the favours of his lord.

THOMAS HARDY

A Wife in London

I

She sits in the tawny vapour
    That the Thames-side lanes have uprolled,
    Behind whose webby fold on fold
Like a waning taper
    The street-lamp glimmers cold.

A messenger's knock cracks smartly,
    Flashed news is in her hand
    Of meaning it dazes to understand
Though shaped so shortly:
    He–has fallen – in the far South Land. . . .

II

'Tis the morrow; the fog hangs thicker,
    The postman nears and goes:
    A letter is brought whose lines disclose
By the firelight flicker
    His hand, whom the worm now knows:

Fresh – firm – penned in highest feather –
    Page-full of his hoped return,
    And of home-planned jaunts by brake and burn
In the summer weather,
    And of new love that they would learn.

LOUIS MACNEICE

London Rain

The rain of London pimples
The ebony street with white
And the neon-lamps of London
Stain the canals of night
And the park becomes a jungle
In the alchemy of night.

My wishes turn to violent
Horses black as coal –
The randy mares of fancy,
The stallions of the soul –
Eager to take the fences
That fence about my soul.

Across the countless chimneys
The horses ride and across
The country to the channel
Where warning beacons toss,
To a place where God and No-God
Play at pitch and toss.

Whichever wins I am happy
For God will give me bliss
But No-God will absolve me
From all I do amiss
And I need not suffer conscience
If the world was made amiss.

Under God we can reckon
On pardon when we fall
But if we are under No-God
Nothing will matter at all,
Arson and rape and murder
Must count for nothing at all.

So reinforced by logic
As having nothing to lose
My lust goes riding horseback
To ravish where I choose,
To burgle all the turrets
Of beauty as I choose.

But now the rain gives over
Its dance upon the town,
Logic and lust together
Come dimly tumbling down,
And neither God nor No-God
Is either up or down.

The argument was wilful,
The alternatives untrue,
We need no metaphysics
To sanction what we do
Or to muffle us in comfort
From what we did not do.

Whether the living river
Began in bog or lake,
The world is what was given,
The world is what we make
And we only can discover
Life in the life we make.

So let the water sizzle
Upon the gleaming slates,
There will be sunshine after
When the rain abates
And rain returning duly
When the sun abates.

My wishes now come homeward,
Their gallopings in vain,
Logic and lust are quiet,
Once more it starts to rain.
Falling asleep I listen
To the falling London rain.

Miss Hamilton in London

It would not be true to say she was doing nothing:
She visited several bookshops, spent an hour
In the Victoria and Albert Museum (Indian section),
And walked carefully through the streets of Kensington
Carrying five mushrooms in a paper bag,
A tin of black pepper, a literary magazine,
And enough money to pay the rent for two weeks.
The sky was cloudy, leaves lay on the pavements.

Nor did she lack human contacts: she spoke
To three shop-assistants and a newsvendor,
And returned the 'Goodnight' of a museum attendant.
Arriving home, she wrote a letter to someone
In Canada, as it might be, or in New Zealand,
Listening to the news as she cooked her meal,
And conversed for five minutes with the landlady.
The air was damp with the mist of late autumn.

A full day, and not unrewarding.
Night fell at the usual seasonal hour.
She drew the curtains, switched on the electric fire,
Washed her hair and read until it was dry,
Then went to bed; where, for the hours of darkness,
She lay pierced by thirty black spears
And felt her limbs numb, her eyes burning,
And dark rust carried along her blood.

W. S. GRAHAM

The Night City

Unmet at Euston in a dream
Of London under Turner's steam
Misting the iron gantries, I
Found myself running away
From Scotland into the golden city.

I ran down Gray's Inn Road and ran
Till I was under a black bridge.
This was me at nineteen
Late at night arriving between
The buildings of the City of London.

And then I (O I have fallen down)
Fell in my dream beside the Bank
Of England's wall to bed, me
With my money belt of Northern ice.
I found Eliot and he said yes

And sprang into a Holmes cab.
Boswell passed me in the fog
Going to visit Whistler who
Was with John Donne who had just seen
Paul Potts shouting on Soho Green.

Midnight. I hear the moon
Light chiming on St Paul's.

The City is empty. Night
Watchmen are drinking their tea.

The Fire had burnt out.
The Plague's pits had closed
And gone into literature.

Between the big buildings
I sat like a flea crouched
In the stopped works of a watch.

from *Annus Mirabilis 1667*

293
Methinks already from this chemic flame
I see a city of more precious mould,
Rich as the town which gives the Indies name,
  With silver paved and all divine with gold.
  Mexico.

294
Already, labouring with a mighty fate,
  She shakes the rubbish from her mounting brow
And seems to have renewed her charter's date,
  Which heav'n will to the death of time allow.

295
More great than human, now, and more *august*,
  New deified she from her fires does rise:
Her widening streets on new foundations trust,
  And, opening, into larger parts she flies.
  Augusta, the old name of London.

296
Before, she like some shepherdess did show,
  Who sat to bathe her by a river's side:
Not answering to her fame, but rude and low,
  Nor taught the beauteous arts of modern pride.

297
Now, like a maiden queen, she will behold
  From her high turrets hourly suitors come:
The East with incense and the West with gold
  Will stand like suppliants to receive her doom.

298

The silver Thames, her own domestic flood,
  Shall bear her vessels like a sweeping train;
And often wind (as of his mistress proud)
  With longing eyes to meet her face again.

299

The wealthy Tagus and the wealthier Rhine
  The glory of their towns no more shall boast:
And Seine, that would with Belgian rivers join,
  Shall find her lustre stained and traffic lost.

300

The vent'rous merchant, who designed more far
  And touches on our hospitable shore,
Charmed with the splendour of this northern star,
  Shall here unlade him and depart no more.

SEAMUS HEANEY

District and Circle

Tunes from a tin whistle underground
Curled up a corridor I'd be walking down
To where I knew I was always going to find
My watcher on the tiles, cap by his side,
His fingers perked, his two eyes eyeing me
In an unaccusing look I'd not avoid,
Or not just yet, since both were out to see
For ourselves.
          As the music larked and capered
I'd trigger and untrigger a hot coin
Held at the ready, but now my gaze was lowered
For was our traffic not in recognition?
Accorded passage, I would re-pocket and nod,
And he, still eyeing me, would also nod.

Posted, eyes front, along the dreamy ramparts
Of escalators ascending and descending
To a monotonous slight rocking in the works,
We were moved along, upstanding.
Elsewhere, underneath, an engine powered,
Rumbled, quickened, evened, quieted.
The white tiles gleamed. In passages that flowed
With draughts from cooler tunnels, I missed the light
Of all-overing, long since mysterious day,
Parks at lunchtime where the sunners lay
On body-heated mown grass regardless,
A resurrection scene minutes before
The resurrection, habitués
Of their garden of delights, of staggered summer.

Another level down, the platform thronged.
I re-entered the safety of numbers,
A crowd half straggle-ravelled and half strung
Like a human chain, the pushy newcomers
Jostling and purling underneath the vault,
On their marks to be first through the doors,
Street-loud, then succumbing to herd-quiet . . .
Had I betrayed or not, myself or him?
Always new to me, always familiar,
This unrepentant, now repentant turn
As I stood waiting, glad of a first tremor,
Then caught up in the now-or-never whelm
Of one and all the full length of the train.

Stepping on to it across the gap,
On to the carriage metal, I reached to grab
The stubby black roof-wort and take my stand
From planted ball of heel to heel of hand
As sweet traction and heavy down-slump stayed me.
I was on my way, well girded, yet on edge,
Spot-rooted, buoyed, aloof,
Listening to the dwindling noises off,
My back to the unclosed door, the platform empty;
And wished it could have lasted,
That long between-times pause before the budge
And glaze-over, when any forwardness
Was unwelcome and bodies readjusted,
Blindsided to themselves and other bodies.

So deeper into it, crowd-swept, strap-hanging,
My lofted arm a-swivel like a flail,
My father's glazed face in my own waning
And craning . . .
                        Again the growl
Of shutting doors, the jolt and one-off treble
Of iron on iron, then a long centrifugal
Haulage of speed through every dragging socket.

57

And so by night and day to be transported
Through galleried earth with them, the only relict
Of all that I belonged to, hurtled forward,
Reflecting in a window mirror-backed
By blasted weeping rock-walls.
                                        Flicker-lit.

SEAMUS HEANEY

The Underground

There we were in the vaulted tunnel running,
You in your going-away coat speeding ahead
And me, me then like a fleet god gaining
Upon you before you turned to a reed

Or some new white flower japped with crimson
As the coat flapped wild and button after button
Sprang off and fell in a trail
Between the Underground and the Albert Hall.

Honeymooning, mooning around, late for the Proms,
Our echoes die in that corridor and now
I come as Hansel came on the moonlit stones
Retracing the path back, lifting the buttons

To end up in a draughty lamplit station
After the trains have gone, the wet track
Bared and tensed as I am, all attention
For your step following and damned if I look back.

JOANNA BAILLIE
London

IT is a goodly sight through the clear air,
From Hampstead's heathy height to see at once
England's vast capital in fair expanse,
Towers, belfries, lengthen'd streets, and structures fair.
St Paul's high dome amidst the vassal bands
Of neighb'ring spires, a regal chieftain stands,
And over fields of ridgy roofs appear,
With distance softly tinted, side by side,
In kindred grace, like twain of sisters dear,
The Towers of Westminster, her Abbey's pride;
While, far beyond, the hills of Surrey shine
Through thin soft haze, and show their wavy line.
View'd thus, a goodly sight! but when survey'd
Through denser air when moisten'd winds prevail,
In her grand panoply of smoke array'd,
While clouds aloft in heavy volumes sail,
She is sublime. – She seems a curtain'd gloom
Connecting heaven and earth, – a threat'ning sign of doom.
With more than natural height, rear'd in the sky
'Tis then St Paul's arrests the wondering eye;
The lower parts in swathing mist conceal'd,
The higher through some half spent shower reveal'd,
So far from earth removed, that well, I trow,
Did not its form man's artful structure show,
It might some lofty alpine peak be deem'd,
The eagle's haunt, with cave and crevice seam'd.
Stretch'd wide on either hand, a rugged screen,
In lurid dimness, nearer streets are seen
Like shoreward billows of a troubled main,
Arrested in their rage. Through drizzly rain,

Cataracts of tawny sheen pour from the skies,
Of furnace smoke black curling columns rise,
And many tinted vapours, slowly pass
O'er the wide draping of that pictured mass.

So shows by day this grand imperial town,
And, when o'er all the night's black stole is thrown,
The distant traveller doth with wonder mark
Her luminous canopy athwart the dark,
Cast up, from myriads of lamps that shine
Along her streets in many a starry line: –
He wondering looks from his yet distant road,
And thinks the northern streamers are abroad.
'What hollow sound is that?' approaching near,
The roar of many wheels breaks on his ear.
It is the flood of human life in motion!
It is the voice of a tempestuous ocean!
With sad but pleasing awe his soul is fill'd,
Scarce heaves his breast, and all within is still'd,
As many thoughts and feelings cross his mind, –
Thoughts, mingled, melancholy, undefined,
Of restless, reckless man, and years gone by,
And Time fast wending to Eternity.

WILLIAM WORDSWORTH

St Paul's

Pressed with conflicting thoughts of love and fear
I parted from thee, Friend! and took my way
Through the great City, pacing with an eye
Downcast, ear sleeping, and feet masterless
That were sufficient guide unto themselves,
And step by step went pensively. Now, mark!
Not how my trouble was entirely hushed,
(That might not be) but how by sudden gift,
Gift of Imagination's holy power,
My soul in her uneasiness received
An anchor of stability. It chanced
That while I thus was pacing I raised up
My heavy eyes and instantly beheld,
Saw at a glance in that familiar spot,
A visionary scene – a length of street
Laid open in its morning quietness,
Deep, hollow, unobstructed, vacant, smooth,
And white with winter's purest white, as fair,
As fresh and spotless as he ever sheds
On field or mountain. Moving Form was none
Save here and there a shadowy Passenger,
Slow, shadowy, silent, dusky, and beyond
And high above this winding length of street,
This noiseless and unpeopled avenue,
Pure, silent, solemn, beautiful, was seen
The huge majestic Temple of St Paul
In awful sequestration, through a veil,
Through its own sacred veil of falling snow.

D. H. LAWRENCE

Piccadilly Circus at Night
Street-Walkers

When into the night the yellow light is roused like dust above
    the towns,
Or like a mist the moon has kissed from off a pool in the midst
    of the downs,

Our faces flower for a little hour pale and uncertain along the
    street,
Daisies that waken all mistaken white-spread in expectancy to
    meet

The luminous mist which the poor things wist was dawn
    arriving across the sky,
When dawn is far behind the star the dust-lit town has driven
    so high.

All the birds are folded in a silent ball of sleep,
    All the flowers are faded from the asphalt isle in the sea,
Only we hard-faced creatures go round and round, and keep
    The shores of this innermost ocean alive and illusory.

Wanton sparrows that twittered when morning looked in at
    their eyes
And the Cyprian's pavement-roses are gone, and now it is we
Flowers of illusion who shine in our gauds, make a Paradise
On the shores of this ceaseless ocean, gay birds of the
    town-dark sea.

LAURENCE BINYON

As I Walked Through London

As I walked through London,
The fresh wound burning in my breast,
As I walked through London,
Longing to have forgotten, to harden my heart, and to rest,
A sudden consolation, a softening light
Touched me: the streets alive and bright,
With hundreds each way thronging, on their tide
Received me, a drop in the stream, unmarked, unknown.
And to my heart I cried:
Here can thy trouble find shelter, thy wound be eased!
For see, not thou alone,
But thousands, each with his smart,
Deep-hidden, perchance, but felt in the core of the heart!
And as to a sick man's feverish veins
The full sponge warmly pressed,
Relieves with its burning the burning of forehead and hands,
So, I, to my aching breast,
Gathered the griefs of those thousands, and made them my own;
My bitterest pains
Merged in a tenderer sorrow, assuaged and appeased.

Villages and Towns

Poem from Llanybri

If you come my way that is . . .
Between now and then, I will offer you
A fist full of rock cress fresh from the bank
The valley tips of garlic red with dew
Cooler than shallots, a breath you can swank

In the village when you come. At noon-day
I will offer you a choice bowl of cawl
Served with a 'lover's' spoon and a chopped spray
Of leeks or savori fach, not used now,

In the old way you'll understand. The din
Of children singing through the eyelet sheds
Ringing smith hoops, chasing the butt of hens;
Or I can offer you Cwmcelyn spread

With quartz stones from the wild scratchings of men:
You will have to go carefully with clogs
Or thick shoes for it's treacherous the fen,
The East and West Marshes also have bogs.

Then I'll do the lights, fill the lamp with oil,
Get coal from the shed, water from the well;
Pluck and draw pigeon with crop of green foil
This your good supper from the lime-tree fell.

A sit by the hearth with blue flames rising,
No talk. Just a stare at 'Time' gathering
Healed thoughts, pool insight, like swan sailing
Peace and sound around the home, offering

You a night's rest and my day's energy.
You must come – start this pilgrimage
Can you come? – send an ode or elegy
In the old way and raise our heritage.

T. S. ELIOT

from *Little Gidding*

If you came this way,
Taking the route you would be likely to take
From the place you would be likely to come from,
If you came this way in may time, you would find the hedges
White again, in May, with voluptuary sweetness.
It would be the same at the end of the journey,
If you came at night like a broken king,
If you came by day not knowing what you came for,
It would be the same, when you leave the rough road
And turn behind the pig-sty to the dull façade
And the tombstone. And what you thought you came for
Is only a shell, a husk of meaning
From which the purpose breaks only when it is fulfilled
If at all. Either you had no purpose
Or the purpose is beyond the end you figured
And is altered in fulfilment. There are other places
Which also are the world's end, some at the sea jaws,
Or over a dark lake, in a desert or a city—
But this is the nearest, in place and time,
Now and in England.

If you came this way,
Taking any route, starting from anywhere,
At any time or at any season,
It would always be the same: you would have to put off
Sense and notion. You are not here to verify,
Instruct yourself, or inform curiosity
Or carry report. You are here to kneel
Where prayer has been valid. And prayer is more
Than an order of words, the conscious occupation
Of the praying mind, or the sound of the voice praying.

And what the dead had no speech for, when living,
They can tell you, being dead: the communication
Of the dead is tongued with fire beyond the language of the
    living.
Here, the intersection of the timeless moment
Is England and nowhere. Never and always.

KATHRYN GRAY

Joyrider

Come, hot-wired from the city, down
a one-car lane, over the keystone bridge
that cannot take the headlong rush,
past the parish church where the dead
were married, with your due disregard.

Come, past chrysanthemum baskets
and post office, the adjoining grocer's,
burn the byways, kick up that stereo,
hand fumbling in a glove compartment,
cassette reams spinning out the window.

Come, accelerate forward into pitch
on less than a quarter of a tank left,
as wheels take flight from the ditch,
leave behind the oaks, the sign *Thank you*
for driving considerately through our village.

Come, while those lights come on
within the regularity of their living rooms,
as curtains part, just post-lapsarian,
until now quite unaware that there were
silences, laws observed to be disturbed.

WILLIAM BARNES

Evenen in the Village

Now the light o' the west is a-turn'd to gloom,
  An' the men be at hwome vrom ground;
An' the bells be a-zendèn all down the Coombe
  From tower, their mwoansome sound.
      An' the wind is still,
     An' the house-dogs do bark,
An' the rooks be a-vled to the elems high an' dark,
  An' the water do roar at mill.

An' the flickerèn light drough the window-peäne
  Vrom the candle's dull fleäme do shoot,
An' young Jemmy the smith is a-gone down leäne,
  A-playèn his shrill-vaïced flute.
      An' the miller's man
     Do zit down at his ease
On the seat that is under the cluster o' trees,
  Wi' his pipe an' his cider can.

ANTHONY DUNN

Bournemouth

The full moon on the water is a drive-in movie
no one watches. The steam-windowed car bobs as if afloat;
on the pier the four-legged, four-armed, two-headed freakshow
kneads its own breasts and begs itself to stop, harder, stop;
six kids in a metro, skinning up, wild with the munchies;
a pensioner, slow-eyed, ashy reefer poised at the down-wound
    glass;
the pinafored waitress, staring out, absently touching herself
in the lighted first-floor window of an empty fish restaurant;
and we, four actors, silhouette ourselves on the screen of the sky,
obnoxious as a fat toe-trampler in a cramped cinema.

The audience, familiar as stereotypes,
as troubled by our passing as the sea by a skimmed stone,
ignores the unreeled sand where its own, its true story
is played out quietly by a cast of dumb extras.
Two fishermen cyclopsed in miner's helmets catch nothing
while a monochrome drunk balances on the water's edge,
    miming
a shouting above the din of the surf into his mobile phone.
Suddenly he is dead still, legs apart, canute-small, phone held
    high
as if the argument of the ocean might explain everything
to whoever it is that cannot listen to him speaking.

DON PATERSON

The Sea at Brighton

To move through your half-million furnished hours
as that gull sails through the derelict tearooms
of the West Pier; to know their shadowed realm
as a blink, a second's darkening of the course . . .

The bird heads for the Palace, then skites over
its blank flags, whitewashed domes and campaniles,
vanishes. Today, the shies and stalls
are locked, the gypsies off to bank the silver;

the ghosts have left the ghost train, and are gone
from every pebble, beach-hut, dog and kite
in the blanket absolution of the light
of a November forenoon. It is that long

instant, when all the vacant forms
are cast upon the ground, that hinge in the day
when the world and its black facsimile
lie open like the book of perfect names.

Old stone-grinder, sky-face, pachyderm,
I render them to you. Now let me walk along
those empty roads above your listening.
I write this on the first morning of term

back home from the country of no songs,
between the blue swell and the stony silence
right down where the one thing meets the millions
at the line of speech, the white assuaging tongues.

SEAN O'BRIEN

Amours de Grimsby

When the sway of the exotic overwhelmed
My lyric impulse, I returned
At length to indigence and Grimsby.
On the quay where the fish-train set me down
And pulled away for Trebizond and Cleethorpes
No gift-box of herrings awaited me this time.
After the exhaustion of my early promise
In mannered elaboration of the same few
Arid tropes, I did not find in Grimsby
Girls in states of half-undress awaiting me
When they had got their shopping from the Co-op,
Had their hair done, phoned their sisters,
Read a magazine and thought I was the one.
I was *homo Grimsby*, brought to bed on spec.
When one bar in Grimsby turned into another –
Shelf of scratchings, half-averted clock,
The glassy roar when time was done
And steam rose from the massive sinks
In which the stars of Grimsby might have bathed –
I got my amicable end away
In Grimsby, or I sat on their settees,
My arms outstretched to mothers winding wool.
Therefore I live in Grimsby, cradled
In a fishwife's scarlet arms from dusk
To hobnailed dawn, my tongue awash
With anchovies and Grimsby's bitter Brown.
Mighty Humber's middle passage shrinks
To flooded footprints on a sandbar, each in turn
Inspected by a half-attentive moon. We sit
In smoke-rooms looking out. We know
That Grimsby is the midst of life, the long
Just-opened hour with its cellophane removed,
The modest editorial in which the world

Might change but does not, when the cellars
Empty back their waters, when the tide that comes
Discreetly to the doors enquires for old sake's sake
If this could be the night to sail away. From Grimsby?

True North

Hitching home for the first time, the last leg
being a bummed ride in a cold guard's van
through the unmanned stations to a platform
iced with snow. It's not much to crow about,

the trip from one term at Portsmouth Poly,
all that Falklands business still to come. From there
the village looked stopped; a clutch of houses
in a toy snow-storm with the dust settled

and me ready to stir it, loaded up
with a haul of new facts, half expecting
flags or bunting, a ticker-tape welcome,
a fanfare or a civic reception.

In the Old New Inn two men sat locked
in an arm-wrestle – their one combined fist
dithered like a compass needle. Later,
after Easter, they would ask me outside

for saying Malvinas in the wrong place
at the wrong time, but that night was Christmas
and the drinks were on them. Christmas! At home
I hosted a new game: stretch a tissue

like a snare drum over a brandy glass,
put a penny on, spark up, then take turns
to dimp burning cigs through the diaphragm
before the tissue gives, the penny drops.

As the guests yawned their heads off I lectured
about wolves: how they mass on the shoreline
of Bothnia, wait for the weather, then
make the crossing when the Gulf heals over.

TONY HARRISON

Illuminations

I

The two machines on Blackpool's Central Pier,
The Long Drop and *The Haunted House* gave me
my thrills the holiday that post-war year
but my father watched me spend impatiently:

Another tanner's worth, but then no more!

But I sneaked back the moment that you napped.
50 weeks of ovens, and 6 years of war
made you want sleep and ozone, and you snapped:

Bugger the machines! Breathe God's fresh air!

I sulked all week, and wouldn't hold your hand.
I'd never heard you mention God, or swear,
and it took me until now to understand.

I see now all the piled old pence turned green,
enough to hang the murderer all year
and stare at millions of ghosts in the machine –

The penny dropped in time! Wish you were here!

II

We built and bombed Boche stalags on the sands,
or hunted for beached starfish on the rocks
and some days ended up all holding hands
gripping the pier machine that gave you shocks.
The current would connect. We'd feel the buzz
ravel our loosening ties to one tense grip,
the family circle, one continuous US!
That was the first year on my scholarship

78

and I'd be the one who'd make that circuit short.
I lectured them on neutrons and Ohm's Law
and other half-baked Physics I'd been taught.
I'm sure my father felt I was a bore!

Two dead, but current still flows through us three
though the circle takes for ever to complete –
eternity, annihilation, me,
that small bright charge of life where they both meet.

EDWIN MUIR

The Wayside Station

Here at the wayside station, as many a morning,
I watch the smoke torn from the fumy engine
Crawling across the field in serpent sorrow.
Flat in the east, held down by stolid clouds,
The struggling day is born and shines already
On its warm hearth far off. Yet something here
Glimmers along the ground to show the seagulls
White on the furrows' black unturning waves.

But now the light has broadened.
I watch the farmstead on the little hill,
That seems to mutter: 'Here is day again'
Unwillingly. Now the sad cattle wake
In every byre and stall,
The ploughboy stirs in the loft, the farmer groans
And feels the day like a familiar ache
Deep in his body, though the house is dark.
The lovers part
Now in the bedroom where the pillows gleam
Great and mysterious as deep hills of snow,
An inaccessible land. The wood stands waiting
While the bright snare slips coil by coil around it,
Dark silver on every branch. The lonely stream
That rode through darkness leaps the gap of light,
Its voice grown loud, and starts its winding journey
Through the day and time and war and history.

Duddingston

I

With caws and chirrupings, the woods
  In this thin sun rejoice,
The Psalm seems but the little kirk
  That sings with its own voice.

The cloud-rifts share their amber light
  With the surface of the mere –
I think the very stones are glad
  To feel each other near.

Once more my whole heart leaps and swells
  And gushes o'er with glee:
The fingers of the sun and shade
  Touch music stops in me.

II

Now fancy paints that bygone day
  When you were here, my fair –
The whole lake rang with rapid skates
  In the windless, winter air.

You leaned to me, I leaned to you,
  Our course was smooth as flight –
We steered – a heel-touch to the left,
  A heel-touch to the right.

We swung our way through flying men,
  Your hand lay fast in mine,
We saw the shifting crowd dispart,
  The level ice-reach shine.

I swear by yon swan-travelled lake,
  By yon calm hill above,
I swear had we been drowned that day
  We had been drowned in love.

JOHN BURNSIDE

The Men's Harbour
(Late November, Anstruther)

The eider are back
          Formal as decoys
they sit at the end of the quay
in the day's first warmth;
Sunday: when the townsmen bring their sons
to fish off the dock,
their rods propped by the wall, the tensed lines
streaming with light;
the boys in hats and scarves and brightly-coloured
anoraks; the men
sober, reflective; wrapped in the quiet of work
that is theirs, for once, and unaccountable

and I can't help but think
there is something they want to pass on:
a knowledge they can't quite voice though it has to do
with the grace that distinguishes strength
from power.
          Beyond the quay,
a crew of gulls is shredding refuse sacks
for morsels of fishbone, choice
oozings of yoghurt or mango.
They half co-operate, half
vie with one another, butting in
for fatter scraps, then fluttering away,
tracking the tarmac with newsprint and crusted grease.

There's nothing elegant in this, no special skill,
nothing save luck and speed and the odd
flutter of threat: a clownish, loud
bravado.
          Further upshore,

the sun finds the white on white
of the caravan park:
blisters of paint and distemper flaking away
from brickwork and metal;
alleys of half-kept garden between the stands;
the scalped grass dusted with frost; a single blackbird
scratching for grubs in the dirt of the island bed.

Someone has set a flag above the dock;
a thin old man in a jerkin and fingerless gloves
mending a hull, his tight lips crammed with nails,
his eyes like shells,
and others here are working on their dreams
of water: men in overalls or coats,
or muddled sweaters, scabbed with paint and rust.
Their hands are dark with oil or coiled in rope;
their bodies subtle, verging on the edge
of weightlessness; no law to hold them here,
no harboured rage.

This is the life they want, their chosen craft,
working with hooks and chains through the
        sea-water-cold.
Each of them knows what it is
to have been refused,
to feel the silence swelling in their throats
and nothing to be said, lest they admit
how little they care for anything but this,
wanting a life that stays
untraceable.
                Each of them knows
and each of them makes his peace:
the burden of a given name and place
discarded in a moment's self-forgetting.

U . A . FANTHORPE

At Swarkestone

'It is often said that Bonnie Prince Charlie got as far as Derby
in his invasion of 1745. In fact, he reached Swarkestone, some
nine miles further south.'

J. G. Collingwood, *The River Trent*

He turned back here. Anyone would. After
The long romantic journey from the North
To be faced with this. A *so what?* sort of place,
A place that, like a mirror, makes you see.

A scrubby ridge, impassive river, and beyond,
The flats of Middle England. History waited
To absorb him. Parliaments, dynasties, empires
Lay beyond these turnip fields. Not what he wanted.

He could have done it. The German Royals
Had packed their bags, there was a run
On the Bank of England, London stood open as jelly.
Nobody could have stopped him. This place did,

And the hurricane that blew his cause from Moidart
In a bluster of kilts and claymores and bright red hair
Faded at Swarkestone as they turned their backs,
Withdrawing into battle, slaughter, song.

DALJIT NAGRA

Parade's End

Dad parked our Granada, champagne-gold
by our superstore on Blackstock Road,
my brother's eyes scanning the men
who scraped the pavement frost to the dole,
one 'got on his bike' over the hill
or the few who warmed us a thumbs-up
for the polished recovery of our re-sprayed car.

Council mums at our meat display
nestled against a pane with white trays
swilling kidneys, liver and a sandy block
of corned beef, loud enough about the way
darkies from down south *Come op ta
Yorksha, mekkin claaims on aut theh can
befoh buggrin off in theh flash caahs!*

At nine, we left the emptied till open,
clicked the dials of the safe. Bolted
two metal bars across the back door
(with a new lock). Spread trolleys
at ends of the darkened aisles. Then we pressed
the code for the caged alarm and rushed
the precinct to check it was throbbing red.

Thundering down the graffiti of shutters
against the valley of high-rise flats.
Ready for the getaway to our cul-de-sac'd
semi-detached, until we stood stock-still:
watching the car-skin pucker, bubbling smarts
of acid. In the unstoppable pub-roar
from the John O'Gaunt across the forecourt,
we returned up to the shop, lifted a shutter,
queued at the sink, walked down again.

Three of us, each carrying pans of cold water.
Then we swept away the bonnet-leaves
from gold to the brown of our former colour.

GEORGE CRABBE

from *The Village: Book I*

The Village Life, and every care that reigns
O'er youthful peasants and declining swains;
What labour yields, and what, that labour past,
Age, in its hour of languor, finds at last;
What form the real picture of the poor,
Demand a song – the Muse can give no more.
  Fled are those times, when, in harmonious strains,
The rustic poet praised his native plains:
No shepherds now, in smooth alternate verse,
Their country's beauty or their nymphs' rehearse;
Yet still for these we frame the tender strain,
Still in our lays fond Corydons complain,
And shepherds' boys their amorous pains reveal,
The only pains, alas! they never feel.
  On Mincio's banks, in Cæsar's bounteous reign,
If Tityrus found the Golden Age again,
Must sleepy bards the flattering dream prolong,
Mechanic echoes of the Mantuan song?
From Truth and Nature shall we widely stray,
Where Virgil, not where Fancy, leads the way?
  Yes, thus the Muses sing of happy swains,
Because the Muses never knew their pains:
They boast their peasants' pipes; but peasants now
Resign their pipes and plod behind the plough;
And few, amid the rural-tribe, have time
To number syllables, and play with rhyme;
Save honest Duck, what son of verse could share
The poet's rapture, and the peasant's care?
Or the great labours of the field degrade,
With the new peril of a poorer trade?
  From this chief cause these idle praises spring,
That themes so easy few forbear to sing;

For no deep thought the trifling subjects ask;
To sing of shepherds is an easy task:
The happy youth assumes the common strain,
A nymph his mistress, and himself a swain;
With no sad scenes he clouds his tuneful prayer,
But all, to look like her, is painted fair.
   I grant indeed that fields and flocks have charms
For him that grazes or for him that farms;
But when amid such pleasing scenes I trace
The poor laborious natives of the place,
And see the mid-day sun, with fervid ray,
On their bare heads and dewy temples play;
While some, with feebler heads and fainter hearts,
Deplore their fortune, yet sustain their parts:
Then shall I dare these real ills to hide
In tinsel trappings of poetic pride?
   No; cast by Fortune on a frowning coast,
Which neither groves nor happy valleys boast;
Where other cares than those the Muse relates,
And other shepherds dwell with other mates;
By such examples taught, I paint the Cot,
As Truth will paint it, and as Bards will not:
Nor you, ye poor, of letter'd scorn complain,
To you the smoothest song is smooth in vain;
O'ercome by labour, and bow'd down by time,
Feel you the barren flattery of a rhyme?
Can poets soothe you, when you pine for bread,
By winding myrtles round your ruin'd shed?
Can their light tales your weighty griefs o'erpower,
Or glad with airy mirth the toilsome hour?
   Lo! where the heath, with withering brake grown o'er,
Lends the light turf that warms the neighbouring poor;
From thence a length of burning sand appears,
Where the thin harvest waves its wither'd ears;
Rank weeds, that every art and care defy,
Reign o'er the land, and rob the blighted rye:
There thistles stretch their prickly arms afar,
And to the ragged infant threaten war;

There poppies nodding, mock the hope of toil;
There the blue bugloss paints the sterile soil;
Hardy and high, above the slender sheaf,
The slimy mallow waves her silky leaf;
O'er the young shoot the charlock throws a shade,
And clasping tares cling round the sickly blade;
With mingled tints the rocky coasts abound,
And a sad splendour vainly shines around.
So looks the nymph whom wretched arts adorn,
Betray'd by man, then left for man to scorn;
Whose cheek in vain assumes the mimic rose,
While her sad eyes the troubled breast disclose;
Whose outward splendour is but folly's dress,
Exposing most, when most it gilds distress.
    Here joyless roam a wild amphibious race,
With sullen wo display'd in every face;
Who, far from civil arts and social fly,
And scowl at strangers with suspicious eye.
    Here too the lawless merchant of the main
Draws from his plough th'intoxicated swain;
Want only claim'd the labour of the day,
But vice now steals his nightly rest away.
    Where are the swains, who, daily labour done,
With rural games play'd down the setting sun;
Who struck with matchless force the bounding ball,
Or made the pond'rous quoit obliquely fall;
While some huge Ajax, terrible and strong,
Engaged some artful stripling of the throng,
And fell beneath him, foil'd, while far around
Hoarse triumph rose, and rocks return'd the sound?
Where now are these?

CAROL ANN DUFFY

Stafford Afternoons

Only there, the afternoons could suddenly pause
and when I looked up from lacing my shoe
a long road held no one, the gardens were empty,
an ice-cream van chimed and dwindled away.

On the motorway bridge, I waved at windscreens,
oddly hurt by the blurred waves back, the speed.
So I let a horse in the noisy field sponge at my palm
and invented, in colour, a vivid lie for us both.

In a cul-de-sac, a strange boy threw a stone.
I crawled through a hedge into long grass
at the edge of a small wood, lonely and thrilled.
The green silence gulped once and swallowed me whole.

I knew it was dangerous. The way the trees
drew sly faces from light and shade, the wood
let out its sticky breath on the back of my neck,
and flowering nettles gathered spit in their throats.

Too late. *Touch*, said the long-haired man
who stood, legs apart, by a silver birch
with a living, purple root in his hand. The sight
made sound rush back; birds, a distant lawnmower,

his hoarse, frightful endearments as I backed away
then ran all the way home; into a game
where children scattered and shrieked
and time fell from the sky like a red ball.

JOHN CLARE

The Village Boy

Free from the cottage corner see how wild
The village boy along the pastures hies
With every smell and sound and sight beguiled
That round the prospect meets his wondering eyes
Now stooping eager for the cowslip peeps
As though he'd get them all – now tired of these
Accross the flaggy brook he eager leaps
For some new flower his happy rapture sees
Now tearing mid the bushes on his knees
Or woodland banks for bluebell flowers he creeps
And now while looking up among the trees
He spies a nest and down he throws his flowers
And up he climbs with new-fed extacies
The happiest object in the summer hours

THOMAS GRAY

Elegy Written in a Country Churchyard

The curfew tolls the knell of parting day,
  The lowing herd wind slowly o'er the lea,
The plowman homeward plods his weary way,
  And leaves the world to darkness and to me.

Now fades the glimmering landscape on the sight,
  And all the air a solemn stillness holds,
Save where the beetle wheels his droning flight,
  And drowsy tinklings lull the distant folds.

Save that from yonder ivy-mantled tower
  The moping owl does to the moon complain
Of such as, wandering near her secret bower,
  Molest her ancient solitary reign.

Beneath those rugged elms, that yew-tree's shade,
  Where heaves the turf in many a mouldering heap,
Each in his narrow cell for ever laid,
  The rude forefathers of the hamlet sleep.

The breezy call of incense-breathing morn,
  The swallow twittering from the straw-built shed,
The cock's shrill clarion, or the echoing horn,
  No more shall rouse them from their lowly bed.

For them no more the blazing hearth shall burn,
  Or busy housewife ply her evening care:
No children run to lisp their sire's return,
  Or climb his knee the envied kiss to share.

Oft did the harvest to their sickle yield,
   Their furrow of the stubborn glebe has broke:
How jocund did they drive their team afield!
   How bowed the woods beneath their sturdy stroke!

Let not ambition mock their useful toil,
   Their homely joys, and destiny obscure;
Nor grandeur hear with a disdainful smile
   The short and simple annals of the poor.

The boast of heraldry, the pomp of power,
   And all that beauty, all that wealth e'er gave,
Awaits alike the inevitable hour.
   The paths of glory lead but to the grave.

Nor you, ye proud, impute to these the fault,
   If memory o'er their tomb no trophies raise,
Where through the long-drawn aisle and fretted vault
   The pealing anthem swells the note of praise.

Can storied urn or animated bust
   Back to its mansion call the fleeting breath?
Can honour's voice provoke the silent dust,
   Or flattery soothe the dull cold ear of death?

Perhaps in this neglected spot is laid
   Some heart once pregnant with celestial fire;
Hands, that the rod of empire might have swayed,
   Or waked to extasy the living lyre.

But knowledge to their eyes her ample page
   Rich with the spoils of time did ne'er unroll;
Chill penury repressed their noble rage,
   And froze the genial current of the soul.

Full many a gem of purest ray serene,
   The dark unfathomed caves of ocean bear;
Full many a flower is born to blush unseen,
   And waste its sweetness on the desert air.

Some village-Hampden, that with dauntless breast
　The little tyrant of his fields withstood,
Some mute inglorious Milton here may rest,
　Some Cromwell guiltless of his country's blood.

The applause of listening senates to command.
　The threats of pain and ruin to despise,
To scatter plenty o'er a smiling land,
　And read their history in a nation's eyes,

Their lot forbad: nor circumscribed alone
　Their growing virtues, but their crimes confined;
Forbad to wade through slaughter to a throne,
　And shut the gates of mercy on mankind,

The struggling pangs of conscious truth to hide,
　To quench the blushes of ingenuous shame,
Or heap the shrine of luxury and pride
　With incense kindled at the Muse's flame.

Far from the madding crowd's ignoble strife,
　Their sober wishes never learned to stray;
Along the cool sequestered vale of life
　They kept the noiseless tenor of their way.

Yet even those bones from insult to protect
　Some frail memorial still erected nigh,
With uncouth rhymes and shapeless sculpture decked,
　Implores the passing tribute of a sigh.

Their name, their years, spelt by the unlettered Muse,
　The place of fame and elegy supply:
And many a holy text around she strews,
　That teach the rustic moralist to die.

For who, to dumb forgetfulness a prey,
　This pleasing anxious being e'er resigned,
Left the warm precincts of the cheerful day,
　Nor cast one longing lingering look behind?

On some fond breast the parting soul relies,
  Some pious drops the closing eye requires;
E'en from the tomb the voice of nature cries,
  E'en in our ashes live their wonted fires.

For thee, who mindful of the unhonoured dead,
  Dost in these lines their artless tale relate;
If chance, by lonely contemplation led,
  Some kindred spirit shall inquire thy fate –

Haply some hoary-headed swain may say,
  'Oft have we seen him at the peep of dawn
Brushing with hasty steps the dews away
  To meet the sun upon the upland lawn.

'There at the foot of yonder nodding beech,
  That wreathes its old fantastic roots so high,
His listless length at noontide would he stretch,
  And pore upon the brook that babbles by.

'Hard by yon wood, now smiling as in scorn,
  Muttering his wayward fancies he would rove,
Now drooping, woeful-wan, like one forlorn,
  Or crazed with care, or crossed in hopeless love.

'One morn I missed him on the customed hill,
  Along the heath, and near his favourite tree;
Another came; nor yet beside the rill,
  Nor up the lawn, nor at the wood was he:

'The next, with dirges due in sad array
  Slow through the church-way path we saw him borne.
Approach and read (for thou can'st read) the lay,
  Graved on the stone beneath yon aged thorn.'

(There scattered oft, the earliest of the year,
  By hands unseen, are showers of violets found:
The redbreast loves to bill and warble there,
  And little footsteps lightly print the ground.)

The Epitaph

Here rests his head upon the lap of Earth
  A Youth, to Fortune and to Fame unknown.
Fair Science frowned not on his humble birth,
  And Melancholy marked him for her own.

Large was his bounty, and his soul sincere,
  Heaven did a recompense as largely send;
He gave to Misery all he had, a tear,
  He gained from Heaven ('twas all he wished) a friend.

No farther seek his merits to disclose,
  Or draw his frailties from their dread abode,
(There they alike in trembling hope repose,)
  The bosom of his Father and his God.

JOHN BETJEMAN

Slough

Come, friendly bombs, and fall on Slough
It isn't fit for humans now,
There isn't grass to graze a cow
   Swarm over, Death!

Come, bombs, and blow to smithereens
Those air-conditioned, bright canteens,
Tinned fruit, tinned meat, tinned milk, tinned beans
   Tinned minds, tinned breath.

Mess up the mess they call a town—
A house for ninety-seven down
And once a week a half-a-crown
   For twenty years,

And get that man with double chin
Who'll always cheat and always win,
Who washes his repulsive skin
   In women's tears,

And smash his desk of polished oak
And smash his hands so used to stroke
And stop his boring dirty joke
   And make him yell.

But spare the bald young clerks who add
The profits of the stinking cad;
It's not their fault that they are mad,
   They've tasted Hell.

It's not their fault they do not know
The birdsong from the radio,
It's not their fault they often go
    To Maidenhead

And talk of sports and makes of cars
In various bogus Tudor bars
And daren't look up and see the stars
    But belch instead.

In labour-saving homes, with care
Their wives frizz out peroxide hair
And dry it in synthetic air
    And paint their nails.

Come, friendly bombs, and fall on Slough
To get it ready for the plough.
The cabbages are coming now;
    The earth exhales.

STEPHEN SPENDER

The Landscape Near an Aerodrome

More beautiful and soft than any moth
With burring furred antennae feeling its huge path
Through dusk, the air-liner with shut-off engines
Glides over suburbs and the sleeves set trailing tall
To point the wind. Gently, broadly, she falls
Scarcely disturbing charted currents of air.

Lulled by descent, the travellers across sea
And across feminine land indulging its easy limbs
In miles of softness, now let their eyes trained by watching
Penetrate through dusk the outskirts of this town
Here where industry shows a fraying edge.
Here they may see what is being done.

Beyond the winking masthead light
And the landing-ground, they observe the outposts
Of work: chimneys like lank black fingers
Or figures, frightening and mad: and squat buildings
With their strange air behind trees, like women's faces
Shattered by grief. Here where few houses
Moan with faint light behind their blinds
They remark the unhomely sense of complaint, like a dog
Shut out, and shivering at the foreign moon.

In the last sweep of love, they pass over fields
Behind the aerodrome, where boys play all day
Hacking dead grass: whose cries, like wild birds,
Settle upon the nearest roofs
But soon are hid under the loud city.

Then, as they land, they hear the tolling bell
Reaching across the landscape of hysteria
To where, louder than all those batteries,
And charcoaled towers against that dying sky,
Religion stands, the church blocking the sun.

JOSEPH BRODSKY
(translated by Alan Myers)

from *In England*
Stone Villages

The stone-built villages of England.
A cathedral bottled in a pub window.
Cows dispersed across the fields.
Monuments to kings.

A man in a moth-eaten suit
sees a train off, heading, like everything here, for the sea,
smiles at his daughter, leaving for the East.
A whistle blows.

And the endless sky over the tiles
grows bluer as swelling birdsong fills.
And the clearer the song is heard,
the smaller the bird.

EDWARD THOMAS

Adlestrop

Yes, I remember Adlestrop –
The name, because one afternoon
Of heat the express-train drew up there
Unwontedly. It was late June.

The steam hissed. Someone cleared his throat.
No one left and no one came
On the bare platform. What I saw
Was Adlestrop – only the name

And willows, willow-herb, and grass,
And meadowsweet, and haycocks dry,
No whit less still and lonely fair
Than the high cloudlets in the sky.

And for that minute a blackbird sang
Close by, and round him, mistier,
Farther and farther, all the birds
Of Oxfordshire and Gloucestershire.

IVOR GURNEY

Tewkesbury

Some Dane looking out from the water-settlements,
If settlements there were, must have thought as I,
'Square stone should fill that bit of lower sky.
Were I a king and had my influence,
Farms should go up for this, flames make terror go high.
But I would set my name in high eminence.'
Forthampton walking, thinking and looking to Tewkesbury
Where a cricketer was born and a battle raged desperate,
And mustard grew, and Stratford boys early or late
May have come, and rivers, green Avon, brown Severn, meet.
And Norman Milo set a seal on the plain –
'Here man rules; his works to be found here;
Acknowledges supremacy, his strengths to be in vain;
And gathers by a sign the broad meadows in round here.'

What is best of England, going quick from beauty,
Is manifest, the slow spirit going straight on,
The dark intention corrected by eyes that see,
The somehow getting there, the last conception
Bettered, and something of one's own spirit outshown;
Grown as oaks grow, done as hard things are done.

Of worthy towns worthy should be Messenger
Of News that's food to heart of Everyman,
The curious of his kind. And on this birthday,
This twice a hundred mark of age and honour,
Well do we salute 'Journal' of Land's fame;
That's gossip to our region villages,
And Record to the Merchant with his lad,
Art's Table and the Tale of Sport and Stage.
Those country folk that stare to see the queer
Rough-textured first-of-kind, have often taken
Their whole week's thought from 'Journal's' gathering-in,

Severn and Vale alike, and known our England,
Europe, the wider world, from that respected
Close-ordered print; and we in hacked-up Flanders
Read Sunday School, Fairs, football-scores alike.
(Raikes, that kind-thoughted, gay man, had laughed,
We sitting there in drips of rain to ponder
On small home businesses, so mired and chill.)
Well to the sober, beautiful city serves
This grave news-printing, old in praise as years,
Looked for at week-ends; worthy of that first
Director, whom in London surprised one sees
Smile from the dun wall on the curious.

But he, could return be, having heard the presses
And thunderous printing, seen and grasped so much,
By fumbling questions groping near the truth,
Would yet have asked what thought the townsfolk had,
This 'Journal', how it stood yet in their minds;
And, answered, should indeed be well content.

Towns are not often lucky in their print-sheets;
But this, the Roman City, has for servant
A Teller wise of grave news-currency.

PAUL HENRY

The Village, a State of Untruth . . .

The village, a state of untruth,
a blunt tongue in a butcher's shop,
the warp in a time-scrubbed block.
You have come back to what never was.
For *Please Drive Carefully*, read
Enter At Your Own Risk.
The churchyard understudies the pub.
The stone wall of the school divides them.
Like wool on a thorn, its name
clings, like unwanted love.
A stranglehold on its youth
lies broken in each grave.
There is no clock, only a stream,
an overhead cheese-wire's hum.
And perhaps you are dreaming this.
Would it not have been safer
to preserve it for suburban friends
on a wall, or in that sheep's skull
next to the fruit on the sideboard?
The village's collective mind
has settled itself in the lull
between question and answer.
Its memory is long.
It haunts, like the heart
cut for the butcher's son
still there on the old yew,
or the map of blood
that clung to his apron
the summer he almost broke free.

from *Gwalia Deserta (XXVI)*

The village of Fochriw grunts among the higher hills;
The dwelling of miners and pigeons and pigs
Cluster around the little grey war memorial.
The sun brings glitter to the long street roofs
And the crawling promontories of slag,
The sun makes the pitwheels to shine,
And praise be to the sun, the great unselfish sun,
The sun that shone on Plato's shoulders,
That dazzles with light the Taj Mahal.
The same sun shone on the first mineowner,
On the vigorous builder of this brown village,
And praise be to the impartial sun.
He had no hand in the bruising of valleys,
He had no line in the vigorous builder's plans,
He had no voice in the fixing of wages,
He was the blameless one.
And he smiles on the village this morning,
He smiles on the far-off grave of the vigorous builder,
On the ivied mansion of the first mineowner,
On the pigeon lofts and the Labour Exchange,
And he smiles as only the innocent can.

HENRY VAUGHAN

from *To His Retired Friend,* *an Invitation to Brecknock*

Since last we met, thou and thy horse (my dear),
Have not so much as drunk, or littered here,
I wonder, though thy self be thus deceased,
Thou hast the spite to coffin up thy beast;
Or is the *palfrey* sick, and his rough hide
With the penance of *one spur* mortified?
Or taught by thee (like *Pythagoras's ox*)
Is than his master grown more *orthodox*?
What ever 'tis, a sober cause't must be
That thus long bars us of thy company.
The town believes thee lost, and didst thou see
But half her sufferings, now distressed for thee,
Thou'ldst swear (like *Rome*) her foul, polluted walls
Were sacked by *Brennus*, and the savage *Gauls*.
Abominable face of things! here's noise
Of banged mortars, blue aprons, and boys,
Pigs, dogs, and drums, with the hoarse hellish notes
Of politicly-deaf usurers' throats,
With new fine *Worships*, and the old cast *team*
Of Justices vexed with the *cough*, and *phlegm*.
Midst these the *Cross* looks sad, and in the *Shire-Hall*
furs of an old *Saxon Fox* appear,
With brotherly ruffs and beards, and a strange sight
Of high monumental hats ta'en at the fight
Of *Eighty-eight*; while every *Burgess* foots
The mortal *pavement* in eternal boots.
   Hadst thou been bach'lor, I had soon divined
Thy close retirements, and monastic mind,
Perhaps some nymph had been to visit, or
The beauteous churl was to be waited for,
And like the *Greek*, ere you the sport would miss

You stayed, and stroked the *distaff* for a kiss.
But in this age, when thy cool, settled blood
Is tied t'one flesh, and thou almost grown good,
I know not how to reach the strange device,
Except (*Domitian* like) thou murderest flies;
Or is't thy piety? for who can tell
But thou mayst prove devout, and love a cell,
And (like a badger) with attentive looks
In the dark hole sit rooting up of books.
Quick hermit! what a peaceful change hadst thou
Without the noise of *hair-cloth*, *whip*, or *vow*?
But is there no redemption? must there be
No other penance but of liberty?
Why two months hence, if thou continue thus
Thy memory will scarce remain with us,
The drawers have forgot thee, and exclaim
They have not seen thee here since *Charles* his reign,
Or if they mention thee, like some old man
That at each word inserts – Sir, *as I can*
Remember – So the *cypherers* puzzle me
With a dark, cloudy character of thee.
That (certs!) I fear thou wilt be lost, and we
Must ask the *fathers* ere't be long for thee.
  Come! leave this sullen state, and let not wine
And precious wit lie dead for want of thine,
Shall the dull *Market-land-lord* with his *rout*
Of sneaking tenants dirtily swill out
This harmless liquor? shall they knock and beat
For sack, only to talk of *rye*, and *wheat*?
O let not such preposterous tippling be
In our *Metropolis*, may I ne'er see
Such *tavern-sacrilege*, nor lend a line
To weep the *Rapes* and *Tragedy* of wine!
Here lives that *chimic*, quick fire which betrays
Fresh spirits to the blood, and warms our lays,
I have reserved 'gainst thy approach a cup
That were thy Muse stark dead, shall raise her up,
And teach her yet more charming words and skill
Than ever *Celia, Chloris, Astrophil,*

Or any of the threadbare names inspired
Poor rhyming lovers with a *mistress* fired.
Come then! and while the slow icicle hangs
At the stiff thatch, and winter's frosty pangs
Benumb the year, blithe (as of old) let us
'Midst noise and war, of peace, and mirth discuss.
This portion thou wert born for: why should we
Vex at the time's ridiculous misery?
An age that thus hath fooled itself, and will
(Spite of thy teeth and mine) persist so still.
Let's sit then at this *fire*, and while we steal
A revel in the town, let others seal,
Purchase or cheat, and who can, let them pay,
Till those black deeds bring on the darksome day;
Innocent spenders we! a better use
Shall wear out our short lease, and leave the obtuse
Rout to their *husks*; they and their bags at best
Have cares in *earnest*, we care for a *jest*.

DYLAN THOMAS

Poem in October

It was my thirtieth year to heaven
Woke to my hearing from harbour and neighbour wood
    And the mussel pooled and the heron
        Priested shore
        The morning beckon
With water praying and call of seagull and rook
And the knock of sailing boats on the net webbed wall
        Myself to set foot
        That second
    In the still sleeping town and set forth.

My birthday began with the water-
Birds and the birds of the winged trees flying my name
    Above the farms and the white horses
        And I rose
        In rainy autumn
And walked abroad in a shower of all my days.
High tide and the heron dived when I took the road
        Over the border
        And the gates
    Of the town closed as the town awoke.

A springful of larks in a rolling
Cloud and the roadside bushes brimming with whistling
    Blackbirds and the sun of October
        Summery
        On the hill's shoulder,
Here were fond climates and sweet singers suddenly
Come in the morning where I wandered and listened
        To the rain wringing
        Wind blow cold
    In the wood faraway under me.

Pale rain over the dwindling harbour
And over the sea wet church the size of a snail
With its horns through mist and the castle
Brown as owls
But all the gardens
Of spring and summer were blooming in the tall tales
Beyond the border and under the lark full cloud.
There could I marvel
My birthday
Away but the weather turned around.

It turned away from the blithe country
And down the other air and the blue altered sky
Streamed again a wonder of summer
With apples
Pears and red currants
And I saw in the turning so clearly a child's
Forgotten mornings when he walked with his mother
Through the parables
Of sun light
And the legends of the green chapels

And the twice told fields of infancy
That his tears burned my cheeks and his heart moved in mine.
These were the woods the river and sea
Where a boy
In the listening
Summertime of the dead whispered the truth of his joy
To the trees and the stones and the fish in the tide.
And the mystery
Sang alive
Still in the water and singingbirds.

And there could I marvel my birthday
Away but the weather turned around. And the true
Joy of the long dead child sang burning
In the sun.
It was my thirtieth
Year to heaven stood there then in the summer noon

Though the town below lay leaved with October blood.
      O may my heart's truth
         Still be sung
On this high hill in a year's turning.

R. S. THOMAS

The Village

Scarcely a street, too few houses
To merit the title; just a way between
The one tavern and the one shop
That leads nowhere and fails at the top
Of the short hill, eaten away
By long erosion of the green tide
Of grass creeping perpetually nearer
This last outpost of time past.

So little happens; the black dog
Cracking his fleas in the hot sun
Is history. Yet the girl who crosses
From door to door moves to a scale
Beyond the bland day's two dimensions.

Stay, then, village, for round you spins
On slow axis a world as vast
And meaningful as any poised
By great Plato's solitary mind.

PHILIP LARKIN

The Explosion

On the day of the explosion
Shadows pointed towards the pithead:
In the sun the slagheap slept.

Down the lane came men in pitboots
Coughing oath-edged talk and pipe-smoke,
Shouldering off the freshened silence.

One chased after rabbits; lost them;
Came back with a nest of lark's eggs;
Showed them; lodged them in the grasses.

So they passed in beards and moleskins,
Fathers, brothers, nicknames, laughter,
Through the tall gates standing open.

At noon, there came a tremor; cows
Stopped chewing for a second; sun,
Scarfed as in a heat-haze, dimmed.

The dead go on before us, they
Are sitting in God's house in comfort,
We shall see them face to face –

Plain as lettering in the chapels
It was said, and for a second
Wives saw men of the explosion

Larger than in life they managed –
Gold as on a coin, or walking
Somehow from the sun towards them,

One showing the eggs unbroken.

GILLIAN CLARKE

Blaen Cwrt

You ask how it is. I will tell you.
There is no glass. The air spins in
The stone rectangle. We warm our hands
With apple wood. Some of the smoke
Rises against the ploughed, brown field
As a sign to our neighbours in the
Four folds of the valley that we are in.
Some of the smoke seeps through the stones
Into the barn where it curls like fern
On the walls. Holding a thick root
I press my bucket through the surface
Of the water, lift it brimming and skim
The leaves away. Our fingers curl on
Enamel mugs of tea, like ploughmen.
The stones clear in the rain
Giving their colours. It's not easy.
There are no brochure blues or boiled sweet
Reds. All is ochre and earth and cloud-green
Nettles tasting sour and the smells of moist
Earth and sheep's wool. The wattle and daub
Chimney hood has decayed away, slowly
Creeping to dust, chalking the slate
Floor with stories. It has all the first
Necessities for a high standard
Of civilised living: silence inside
A circle of sound, water and fire,
Light on uncountable miles of mountain
From a big, unpredictable sky,
Two rooms, waking and sleeping,
Two languages, two centuries of past
To ponder on, and the basic need
To work hard in order to survive.

ALAN BROWNJOHN

For a Journey

House Field, Top Field, Oak Field, Third Field:
Though maps conclude their duties, the names trek on
Unseen across every county. Farmers call hillocks
And ponds and streams and lanes and rocks
By the first words to hand; a heavy, whittled-down
Simplicity meets the need, enough to help say
Where has yielded best, or the way they walked from home.

You can travel safely over land so named –
Where there is nowhere that could not somewhere
Be found in a memory which knows, and loves.
So watch then, all the more carefully, for
The point where the pattern ends: where mountains, even,
And swamps and forests and gaping bays acquire
The air of not needing ever to be spoken of.

Who knows what could become of you where
No one has understood the place with names?

Mountains and Moorland

SYLVIA PLATH

Wuthering Heights

The horizons ring me like faggots,
Tilted and disparate, and always unstable.
Touched by a match, they might warm me,
And their fine lines singe
The air to orange
Before the distances they pin evaporate,
Weighting the pale sky with a soldier color.
But they only dissolve and dissolve
Like a series of promises, as I step forward.

There is no life higher than the grasstops
Or the hearts of sheep, and the wind
Pours by like destiny, bending
Everything in one direction.
I can feel it trying
To funnel my heat away.
If I pay the roots of the heather
Too close attention, they will invite me
To whiten my bones among them.

The sheep know where they are,
Browsing in their dirty wool-clouds,
Gray as the weather.
The black slots of their pupils take me in.
It is like being mailed into space,
A thin, silly message.
They stand about in grandmotherly disguise,
All wig curls and yellow teeth
And hard, marbly baas.

I come to wheel ruts, and water
Limpid as the solitudes
That flee through my fingers.

Hollow doorsteps go from grass to grass;
Lintel and sill have unhinged themselves.
Of people and the air only
Remembers a few odd syllables.
It rehearses them moaningly:
Black stone, black stone.

The sky leans on me, me, the one upright
Among all horizontals.
The grass is beating its head distractedly.
It is too delicate
For a life in such company;
Darkness terrifies it.
Now, in valleys narrow
And black as purses, the house lights
Gleam like small change.

'Loud without the wind was roaring'

Loud without the wind was roaring
  Through the waned autumnal sky;
Drenching wet, the cold rain pouring
  Spoke of stormy winters nigh.
    All too like that dreary eve
    Sighed within repining grief;

Sighed at first, but sighed not long –
  Sweet – how softly sweet it came!
Wild words of an ancient song,
  Undefined, without a name.

'It was spring, for the skylark was singing.'
  Those words, they awakened a spell –
They unlocked a deep fountain whose springing
  Nor absence nor distance can quell.

In the gloom of a cloudy November,
  They uttered the music of May;
They kindled the perishing ember
  In fervour that could not decay.

Awaken on all my dear moorlands
  The wind in its glory and pride!
O call me from valleys and highlands
  To walk by the hill-river's side!

It is swelled with the first snowy weather;
  The rocks they are icy and hoar
And darker waves round the long heather
  And the fern-leaves are sunny no more.

There are no yellow-stars on the mountain,
    The blue-bells have long died away
From the brink of the moss-bedded fountain,
    From the side of the wintery brae –

But lovelier than corn-fields all waving
    In emerald and scarlet and gold
Are the slopes where the north-wind is raving,
    And the glens where I wandered of old.

'It was morning; the bright sun was beaming.'
    How sweetly that brought back to me
The time when nor labour nor dreaming
    Broke the sleep of the happy and free.

But blithely we rose as the dusk heaven
    Was melting to amber and blue;
And swift were the wings to our feet given
    While we traversed the meadows of dew,

For the moors, for the moors where the short grass
    Like velvet beneath us should lie!
For the moors, for the moors where each high pass
    Rose sunny against the clear sky!

For the moors where the linnet was trilling
    Its song on the old granite stone;
Where the lark – the wild skylark was filling
    Every breast with delight like its own.

What language can utter the feeling
    That rose when, in exile afar,
On the brow of a lonely hill kneeling
    I saw the brown heath growing there.

It was scattered and stunted, and told me
    That soon even that would be gone;
It whispered, 'The grim walls enfold me;
    I have bloomed in my last summer's sun.'

But not the loved music whose waking
    Makes the soul of the Swiss die away
Has a spell more adored and heart-breaking
    Than in its half-blighted bells lay.

The spirit that bent 'neath its power,
    How it longed, how it burned to be free!
If I could have wept in that hour
    Those tears had been heaven to me.

Well, well, the sad minutes are moving
    Though loaded with trouble and pain;
And sometime the loved and the loving
    Shall meet on the mountains again.

TED HUGHES

Wuthering Heights

Walter was guide. His mother's cousin
Inherited some Brontë soup dishes.
He felt sorry for them. Writers
Were pathetic people. Hiding from it
And making it up. But your transatlantic elation
Elated him. He effervesced
Like his rhubarb wine kept a bit too long:
A vintage of legends and gossip
About those poor lasses. Then,
After the Rectory, after the chaise longue
Where Emily died, and the midget hand-made books,
The elvish lacework, the dwarfish fairy-work shoes,
It was the track from Stanbury. That climb
A mile beyond expectation, into
Emily's private Eden. The moor
Lifted and opened its dark flower
For you too. That was satisfactory.
Wilder, maybe, than ever Emily knew it.
With wet feet and nothing on her head
She trudged that climbing side towards friends –
Probably. Dark redoubt
On the skyline above. It was all
Novel and exhilarating to you.
The book becoming a map. *Wuthering Heights*
Withering into perspective. We got there
And it was all gaze. The open moor,
Gamma rays and decomposing starlight
Had repossessed it
With a kind of blackening smoulder. The centuries
Of door-bolted comfort finally amounted
To a forsaken quarry. The roofs'
Deadfall slabs were flaking, but mostly in place,
Beams and purlins softening. So hard

To imagine the life that had lit
Such a sodden, raw-stone cramp of refuge.
The floors were a rubble of stone and sheep droppings.
Doorframes, windowframes –
Gone to make picnickers' fires or evaporated.
Only the stonework – black. The sky – blue.
And the moor-wind flickering.
                                        The incomings,
The outgoings – how would you take up now
The clench of that struggle? The leakage
Of earnings off a few sickly bullocks
And a scatter of crazed sheep. Being cornered
Kept folk here. Was that crumble of wall
Remembering a try at a garden? Two trees
Planted for company, for a child to play under,
And to have something to stare at. Sycamores –
The girth and spread of valley twenty-year-olds,
They were probably ninety.
                                        You breathed it all in
With jealous, emulous sniffings. Weren't you
Twice as ambitious as Emily? Odd
To watch you, such a brisk pendant
Of your globe-circling aspirations,
Among those burned-out, worn-out remains
Of failed efforts, failed hopes –
Iron beliefs, iron necessities,
Iron bondage, already
Crumbling back to the wild stone.
                                        You perched
In one of the two trees
Just where the snapshot shows you.
Doing as Emily never did. You
Had all the liberties, having life.
The future had invested in you –
As you might say of a jewel
So brilliantly faceted, refracting
Every tint, where Emily had stared
Like a dying prisoner.
And a poem unfurled from you

Like a loose frond of hair from your nape
To be clipped and kept in a book. What would stern
Dour Emily have made of your frisky glances
And your huge hope? Your huge
Mortgage of hope. The moor-wind
Came with its empty eyes to look at you,
And the clouds gazed sidelong, going elsewhere,
The heath-grass, fidgeting in its fever,
Took idiot notice of you. And the stone,
Reaching to touch your hand, found you real
And warm, and lucent, like that earlier one.
And maybe a ghost, trying to hear your words,
Peered from the broken mullions
And was stilled. Or was suddenly aflame
With the scorch of doubled envy. Only
Gradually quenched in understanding.

CLARE POLLARD

The Caravan

We were alive that evening, on the north Yorkshire moors,
in a valley of scuffed hills and smouldering gorse.
Pheasants strutted, their feathers as richly patterned
as Moroccan rugs, past the old Roma caravan –
candles, a rose-cushioned bed, etched glass –
that I'd hired to imagine us gipsies
as our bacon and bean stew bubbled,
as you built a fire, moustached, shirt-sleeves rolled.
It kindled and started to lick, and you laughed
in your muddy boots, there in the wild –
or as close as we can now get to the wild –
skinning up a joint with dirty hands, sloshing wine
into beakers, the sky turning heather with night,
the moon a huge cauldron of light,
the chill wind blasting away our mortgage,
emails, bills, TV, our broken washing machine.
Smoke and stars meant my thoughts loosened,
and took off like the owls that circled overhead,
and I knew your hands would later catch in my hair,
hoped the wedding ring on them never seemed a snare –
for if you were a traveller I would not make you settle,
but would have you follow your own weather,
and if you were a hawk I would not have you hooded,
but would watch, dry-mouthed, as you hung above the fields,
and if you were a rabbit I would not want you tame,
but would watch you gambolling through the bracken,
though there is dark meat packed around your ribs,
and the hawk hangs in the skies.

ROBERT GRAVES

Rocky Acres

This is a wild land, country of my choice,
With harsh craggy mountain, moor ample and bare.
Seldom in these acres is heard any voice
But voice of cold water that runs here and there
Through rocks and lank heather growing without care.
No mice in the heath run, no song-birds fly
For fear of the buzzard that floats in the sky.

He soars and he hovers, rocking on his wings,
He scans his wide parish with a sharp eye,
He catches the trembling of small hidden things,
He tears them in pieces, dropping them from the sky;
Tenderness and pity the heart will deny,
Where life is but nourished by water and rock—
A hardy adventure, full of fear and shock.

Time has never journeyed to this lost land,
Crakeberry and heather bloom out of date,
The rocks jut, the streams flow singing on either hand,
Careless if the season be early or late,
The skies wander overhead, now blue, now slate;
Winter would be known by his cutting snow
If June did not borrow his armour also.

Yet this is my country, beloved by me best,
The first land that rose from Chaos and the Flood,
Nursing no valleys for comfort or rest,
Trampled by no shod hooves, bought with no blood.
Sempiternal country whose barrows have stood
Stronghold for demigods when on earth they go,
Terror for fat burghers on far plains below.

WILLIAM WORDSWORTH
from *The Prelude, Book XIII*
Conclusion

In one of these excursions, travelling then
Through Wales on foot, and with a youthful Friend,
I left Bethkelet's huts at couching-time,
And westward took my way to see the sun
Rise from the top of Snowdon. Having reached
The Cottage at the Mountain's foot, we there
Rouzed up the Shepherd, who by ancient right
Of office is the Stranger's usual Guide,
And after short refreshment sallied forth.

    It was a Summer's night, a close warm night,
Wan, dull and glaring, with a dripping mist
Low-hung and thick that covered all the sky,
Half threatening storm and rain; but on we went
Unchecked, being full of heart and having faith
In our tried Pilot. Little could we see,
Hemmed round on every side with fog and damp,
And, after ordinary travellers' chat
With our Conductor, silently we sank
Each into commerce with his private thoughts.
Thus did we breast the ascent, and by myself
Was nothing either seen or heard the while
Which took me from my musings, save that once
The Shepherd's Cur did to his own great joy
Unearth a hedgehog in the mountain crags
Round which he made a barking turbulent.
This small adventure, for even such it seemed
In that wild place and at the dead of night,
Being over and forgotten, on we wound
In silence as before. With forehead bent
Earthward, as if in opposition set
Against an enemy, I panted up

With eager pace, and no less eager thoughts.
Thus might we wear perhaps an hour away,
Ascending at loose distance each from each,
And I, as chanced, the foremost of the Band;
When at my feet the ground appeared to brighten,
And with a step or two seemed brighter still;
Nor had I time to ask the cause of this,
For instantly a Light upon the turf
Fell like a flash: I looked about, and lo!
The Moon stood naked in the Heavens, at height
Immense above my head, and on the shore
I found myself of a huge sea of mist,
Which, meek and silent, rested at my feet.
A hundred hills their dusky backs upheaved
All over this still Ocean, and beyond,
Far, far beyond, the vapours shot themselves,
In headlands, tongues, and promontory shapes,
Into the Sea, the real Sea, that seemed
To dwindle and give up its majesty,
Usurped upon as far as sight could reach.
Meanwhile, the Moon looked down upon this shew
In single glory, and we stood, the mist
Touching our very feet; and from the shore
At distance not the third part of a mile
Was a blue chasm; a fracture in the vapour,
A deep and gloomy breathing-place, through which
Mounted the roar of waters, torrents, streams
Innumerable, roaring with one voice.
The universal spectacle throughout
Was shaped for admiration and delight,
Grand in itself alone, but in that breach
Through which the homeless voice of waters rose,
That dark deep thoroughfare, had Nature lodged
The Soul, the Imagination of the whole.

A meditation rose in me that night
Upon the lonely Mountain when the scene
Had passed away, and it appeared to me
The perfect image of a mighty Mind,

Of one that feeds upon infinity,
That is exalted by an underpresence,
The sense of God, or whatso'er is dim
Or vast in its own being; above all
One function of such mind had Nature there
Exhibited by putting forth, and that
With circumstance most awful and sublime,
That domination which she oftentimes
Exerts upon the outward face of things,
So moulds them, and endues, abstracts, combines,
Or by abrupt and unhabitual influence
Doth make one object so impress itself
Upon all others, and pervade them so,
That even the grossest minds must see and hear
And cannot chuse but feel.

THOMAS GRAY

The Bard – Pindaric Ode

'Ruin seize thee, ruthless King!
Confusion on thy banners wait!
Tho' fanned by Conquest's crimson wing,
They mock the air with idle state.
Helm, nor hauberk's twisted mail,
Nor e'en thy virtues, Tyrant, shall avail
To save thy secret soul from nightly fears,
From Cambria's curse, from Cambria's tears!'
Such were the sounds that o'er the crested pride
Of the first Edward scattered wild dismay,
As down the steep of Snowdon's shaggy side
He wound with toilsome march his long array.
Stout Glo'ster stood aghast in speechless trance:
'To arms!' cried Mortimer, and couched his quiv'ring lance.

On a rock, whose haughty brow
Frowns o'er cold Conway's foaming flood,
Robed in the sable garb of woe
With haggard eyes the Poet stood;
(Loose his beard and hoary hair
Streamed like a meteor to the troubled air)
And with a master's hand, and prophet's fire,
Struck the deep sorrows of his lyre.
'Hark, how each giant-oak and desert-cave
Sighs to the torrent's awful voice beneath!
O'er thee, O King! their hundred arms they wave,
Revenge on thee in hoarser murmurs breathe;
Vocal no more, since Cambria's fatal day,
To high-born Hoel's harp, or soft Llewellyn's lay.

'Cold is Cadwallo's tongue,
That hushed the stormy main;
Brave Urien sleeps upon his craggy bed:
Mountains, ye mourn in vain
Modred, whose magic song
Made huge Plinlimmon bow his cloud-topt head.
On dreary Arvon's shore they lie,
Smeared with gore, and ghastly pale:
Far, far aloof th'affrighted ravens sail;
The famished eagle screams, and passes by.
Dear lost companions of my tuneful art,
Dear as the light that visits these sad eyes,
Dear as the ruddy drops that warm my heart,
Ye died amidst your dying country's cries –
No more I weep. They do not sleep.
On yonder cliffs, a grisly band,
I see them sit; they linger yet,
Avengers of their native land:
With me in dreadful harmony they join,
And weave with bloody hands the tissue of thy line.

'Weave, the warp! and weave, the woof!
The winding sheet of Edward's race:
Give ample room and verge enough
The characters of hell to trace.
Mark the year and mark the night
When Severn shall re-echo with affright
The shrieks of death, thro' Berkley's roof that ring,
Shrieks of an agonizing king!
She-wolf of France, with unrelenting fangs,
That tear'st the bowels of thy mangled mate,
From thee be born, who o'er thy country hangs
The scourge of Heaven! What terrors round him wait!
Amazement in his van, with Flight combined,
And Sorrow's faded form, and Solitude behind.

'Mighty victor, mighty lord!
Low on his funeral couch he lies!
No pitying heart, no eye, afford
A tear to grace his obsequies.
Is the sable warrior fled?
Thy son is gone. He rests among the dead.
The swarm that in thy noon-tide beam were born?
Gone to salute the rising morn.
Fair laughs the morn, and soft the zephyr blows,
While proudly riding o'er the azure realm
In gallant trim the gilded vessel goes:
Youth on the prow, and Pleasure at the helm:
Regardless of the sweeping whirlwind's sway,
That, hushed in grim repose, expects his ev'ning prey.

'Fill high the sparkling bowl,
The rich repast prepare;
Reft of a crown, he yet may share the feast:
Close by the regal chair
Fell Thirst and Famine scowl
A baleful smile upon their baffled guest.
Heard ye the din of battle bray,
Lance to lance, and horse to horse?
Long years of havoc urge their destined course,
And thro' the kindred squadrons mow their way.
Ye towers of Julius, London's lasting shame,
With many a foul and midnight murder fed,
Revere his consort's faith, his father's fame,
And spare the meek usurper's holy head.
Above, below, the rose of snow,
Twined with her blushing foe, we spread:
The bristled Boar in infant-gore
Wallows beneath the thorny shade.
Now, brothers, bending o'er the accursed loom,
Stamp we our vengeance deep, and ratify his doom.

'Edward, lo! to sudden fate
(Weave we the woof. The thread is spun.)
Half of thy heart we consecrate.
(The web is wove. The work is done.)
Stay, oh stay! nor thus forlorn
Leave me unblessed, unpitied, here to mourn:
In yon bright track that fires the western skies
They melt, they vanish from my eyes.
But oh! what solemn scenes on Snowdon's height
Descending slow their glittering skirts unroll?
Visions of glory, spare my aching sight,
Ye unborn ages, crowd not on my soul!
No more our long-lost Arthur we bewail.
All hail, ye genuine kings! Britannia's issue, hail!

'Girt with many a baron bold
Sublime their starry fronts they rear;
And gorgeous dames, and statesmen old
In bearded majesty, appear.
In the midst a form divine!
Her eye proclaims her of the Briton-line:
Her lion-port, her awe-commanding face,
Attempered sweet to virgin grace.
What strings symphonious tremble in the air,
What strains of vocal transport round her play!
Hear from the grave, great Taliessin, hear;
They breathe a soul to animate thy clay.
Bright Rapture calls, and soaring as she sings,
Waves in the eye of heav'n her many-coloured wings.

'The verse adorn again
Fierce War, and faithful Love,
And Truth severe, by fairy Fiction drest.
In buskined measures move
Pale Grief, and pleasing Pain,
With Horror, tyrant of the throbbing breast.

A voice, as of the cherub-choir,
Gales from blooming Eden bear;
And distant warblings lessen on my ear,
That lost in long futurity expire.
Fond impious man, think'st thou yon sanguine cloud,
Raised by thy breath, has quenched the orb of day?
Tomorrow he repairs the golden flood,
And warms the nations with redoubled ray.
Enough for me: with joy I see
The diff'rent doom our fates assign.
Be thine Despair and sceptred Care;
To triumph and to die are mine.'
He spoke, and headlong from the mountain's height
Deep in the roaring tide he plunged to endless night.

WALDO WILLIAMS
(translated by Tony Conran)

On Weun Cas' Mael

I'll walk once more on Weun Cas' Mael—
And bushes of gorse tell the tale,
Sick withered winter without fail
    Is losing the day.
'Our kindly sky will be blue in a while,'
    Flaming, they say.

Even today, over the drear
Dank moorland, when a moment's clear
A skylark gives its confident cheer,
    Zestful and strong,
Inspiring hope in the country near,
    Unlocks bright song.

Oh, blossom on the roughest tree,
Oh, song on the steep, wild and free—
One sweet from the one strength, to be
    The brave delight
Of bare acres the world can't see
    Or value right.

Wales of dark moorland and stone,
Nurse of the mind that stands alone,
From age to age your strength's been shown
    And still it stays.
Bring us to share in, O make known
    Your life, your ways!

The lovely severity you show
Woke favour of man with man, to grow
A company all one, and so
    By you empowered,
Knowing no slavery, their slow
    Order flowered.

From steel captivity, low hurt
Crosses Cas' Mael. O save us yet!
Men serve the false power in the pit
    Of dark Tre Cŵn.
To the pure breezes, raise us out
    Of the cave's tomb!

As the lark gives from your ground
Point and zest in his circling round,
Your praise let each gift teach to sound,
    Nurture and grow it,
And grant me, Wales, that I be found,
    For your sake, poet.

TED HUGHES

Warm Moors

The moorline fumes like a pane of ice held up to the thawing
    blue.
And the lark, that toad of the roots,
Begins under the ear's moist threshold.

Then out and up, the lung's deep muscle
Building the stair, lifting stone
By stone a stair up the air, taking his time

To score the face of every stone as he sings
With a scoring and scribbling chisel,
This is the way the lark climbs into the sun –

Till your eye's gossamer snaps and your hearing floats back
    widely to earth.

After which the sky lies blank open
Without wings, and the earth is a folded clod.
Only the sun goes silently and endlessly on with the lark's song.

R. S. THOMAS

The Moor

It was like a church to me.
I entered it on soft foot,
Breath held like a cap in the hand.
It was quiet.
What God was there made himself felt,
Not listened to, in clean colours
That brought a moistening of the eye,
In movement of the wind over grass.

There were no prayers said. But stillness
Of the heart's passions – that was praise
Enough; and the mind's cession
Of its kingdom. I walked on.
Simple and poor, while the air crumbled
And broke on me generously as bread.

JOHN CLARE

from *The Moors*

Far spread the moory ground a level scene,
Bespread with rush and one eternal green,
That never felt the rage of blundering plough
Though centuries wreathed Spring's blossoms on its brow,
Still meeting plains that stretched them far away
In unchecked shadows of green, brown and grey.
Unbounded freedom ruled the wandering scene
Nor fence of ownership crept in between
To hide the prospect of the following eye;
Its only bondage was the circling sky.
One mighty flat undwarfed by bush and tree
Spread its faint shadow of immensity
And lost itself, which seemed to eke its bounds,
In the blue mist the horizon's edge surrounds.
Now this sweet vision of my boyish hours,
Free as Spring clouds and wild as Summer flowers,
Is faded all – a hope that blossomed free
And hath been once no more shall ever be.
Enclosure came and trampled on the grave
Of labour's rights and left the poor a slave;
And memory's pride, ere want to wealth did bow,
Is both the shadow and the substance now.
The sheep and cows were free to range as then
Where change might prompt, nor felt the bonds of men.
Cows went and came with evening, morn and night
To the wild pasture as their common right
And sheep, unfolded with the rising sun,
Heard the swains shout and felt their freedom won,
Tracked the red fallow field and heath and plain,
Then met the brook and drank and roamed again –
The brook that dribbled on as clear as glass
Beneath the roots they hid among the grass –

While the glad shepherd traced their tracks along,
Free as the lark and happy as her song.
But now all's fled and flats of many a dye
That seemed to lengthen with the following eye,
Moors losing from the sight, far, smooth and blea,
Where swopt the plover in its pleasure free.
Are vanished now with commons wild and gay
As poets' visions of life's early day . . .
Each little tyrant with his little sign
Shows, where man claims, earth glows no more divine.
On paths to freedom and to childhood dear
A board sticks up to notice 'no road here'
And on the tree with ivy overhung
The hated sign by vulgar taste is hung
As though the very birds should learn to know
When they go there they must no further go.
Thus, with the poor, scared freedom bade good bye
And much they feel it in the smothered sign,
And birds and trees and flowers without a name
All sighed when lawless law's enclosure came;
And dreams of plunder in such rebel schemes
Have found too truly that they were but dreams.

ROBERT BURNS

Farewell to the Highlands

My heart's in the Highlands, my heart is not here;
My heart's in the Highlands a chasing the deer;
A chasing the wild deer, and following the roe,
My heart's in the Highlands, wherever I go.
Farewell to the Highlands, farewell to the north,
The birth place of Valour, the country of Worth,
Wherever I wander, wherever I rove,
The hills of the Highlands for ever I love.

Farewell to the mountains high cover'd with snow;
Farewell to the straths and green vallies below:
Farewell to the forests and wild hanging woods;
Farewell to the torrents and loud pouring floods.
My heart's in the Highlands, my heart is not here,
My heart's in the Highlands, a chasing the deer:
Chasing the wild deer, and following the roe,
My heart's in the Highlands, wherever I go.

Lines Written in the Highlands after a Visit to Burns's Country

There is a joy in footing slow across a silent plain,
Where patriot battle has been fought when glory had the gain;
There is a pleasure on the heath where Druids old have been,
Where mantles grey have rustled by and swept the nettles green;
There is a joy in every spot made known by times of old,
New to the feet, although the tale a hundred times be told;
There is a deeper joy than all, more solemn in the heart,
More parching to the tongue than all, of more divine a smart,
When weary steps forget themselves upon a pleasant turf,
Upon hot sand, or flinty road, or sea-shore iron scurf,
Toward the castle or the cot, where long ago was born
One who was great through mortal days, and died of fame
    unshorn.
Light heather-bells may tremble then, but they are far away;
Wood-lark may sing from sandy fern, the sun may hear his lay;
Runnels may kiss the grass on shelves and shallows clear,
But their low voices are not heard, though come on travels drear;
Blood-red the sun may set behind black mountain peaks;
Blue tides may sluice and drench their time in caves and weedy
    creeks;
Eagles may seem to sleep wing-wide upon the air;
Ring-doves may fly convulsed across to some high-cedared lair;
But the forgotten eye is still fast wedded to the ground,
As palmer's that, with weariness, mid-desert shrine hath found.
At such a time the soul's a child, in childhood is the brain;
Forgotten is the worldly heart – alone, it beats in vain.
Ay, if a madman could have leave to pass a healthful day
To tell his forehead's swoon and faint when first began decay,
He might make tremble many a man whose spirit had gone forth
To find a bard's low cradle-place about the silent North!

Scanty the hour and few the steps beyond the bourn of care,
Beyond the sweet and bitter world – beyond it unaware;
Scanty the hour and few the steps, because a longer stay
Would bar return, and make a man forget his mortal way.
O horrible! to lose the sight of well-remembered face,
Of brother's eyes, of sister's brow, constant to every place,
Filling the air, as on we move, with portraiture intense,
More warm than those heroic tints that fill a painter's sense,
When shapes of old come striding by, and visages of old,
Locks shining black, hair scanty grey, and passions manifold.
No, no, that horror cannot be, for at the cable's length
Man feels the gentle anchor pull and gladdens in its strength –
One hour, half-idiot, he stands by mossy waterfall,
But in the very next he reads his soul's memorial.
He reads it on the mountain's height, where chance he may sit
    down
Upon rough marble diadem, that hill's eternal crown.
Yet be the anchor e'er so fast, room is there for a prayer.
That man may never lose his mind on mountains bleak and bare;
That he may stray league after league some great birth-place to
    find,
And keep his vision clear from speck, his inward sight unblind.

Lachin y Gair

Away, ye gay landscapes, ye gardens of roses!
  In you let the minions of luxury rove;
Restore me the rocks, where the snow-flake reposes.
  Though still they are sacred to freedom and love:
Yet, Caledonia, beloved are thy mountains,
  Round their white summits though elements war;
Though cataracts foam 'stead of smooth-flowing
      fountains,
  I sigh for the valley of dark Loch na Garr.

Ah! there my young footsteps in infancy wander'd;
  My cap was the bonnet, my cloak was the plaid;
On chieftains long perish'd my memory ponder'd,
  As daily I strode through the pine-cover'd glade;
I sought not my home till the day's dying glory
  Gave place to the rays of the bright polar star;
For fancy was cheer'd by traditional story,
  Disclosed by the natives of dark Loch na Garr.

'Shades of the dead! have I not heard your voices
  Rise on the night-rolling breath of the gale?'
Surely the soul of the hero rejoices,
  And rides on the wind, o'er his own Highland vale.
Round Loch na Garr while the stormy mist gathers,
  Winter presides in his cold icy car:
Clouds there encircle the forms of my fathers;
  They dwell in the tempests of dark Loch na Garr.

'Ill-starr'd, though brave, did no visions foreboding
  Tell you that fate had forsaken your cause?'
Ah! were you destined to die at Culloden,
  Victory crown'd not your fall with applause:

146

Still were you happy in death's earthly slumber,
    You rest with your clan in the caves of Braemar;
The pibroch resounds, to the piper's loud number,
    Your deeds on the echoes of dark Loch na Garr.

Years have roll'd on, Loch na Garr, since I left you.
    Years must elapse ere I tread you again:
Nature of verdure and flow'rs has bereft you,
    Yet still are you dearer than Albion's plain.
England! thy beauties are tame and domestic
    To one who has roved o'er the mountains afar:
Oh for the crags that are wild and majestic!
    The steep frowning glories of dark Loch na Garr.

Inversnaid

This darksome burn, horseback brown,
His rollrock highroad roaring down,
In coop and in comb the fleece of his foam
Flutes and low to the lake falls home.

A windpuff-bonnet of fáwn-fróth
Turns and twindles over the broth
Of a pool so pitchblack, féll-frówning,
It rounds and rounds Despair to drowning.

Degged with dew, dappled with dew
Are the groins of the braes that the brook treads through,
Wiry heathpacks, flitches of fern,
And the beadbonny ash that sits over the burn.

What would the world be, once bereft
Of wet and of wilderness? Let them be left,
O let them be left, wildness and wet;
Long live the weeds and the wilderness yet.

EDWIN MUIR

The Mountains

The days have closed behind my back
  Since I came into these hills.
Now memory is a single field
  One peasant tills and tills.

So far away, if I should turn
  I know I could not find
That place again. These mountains make
  The backward gaze half-blind,

Yet sharp my sight till it can catch
  The ranges rising clear
Far in futurity's high-walled land;
  But I am rooted here.

And do not know where lies my way,
  Backward or forward. If I could
I'd leap time's bound or turn and hide
  From time in my ancestral wood.

Double delusion! Here I'm held
  By the mystery of the rock,
Must watch in a perpetual dream
  The horizon's gates unlock and lock,

See on the harvest fields of time
  The mountains heaped like sheaves,
And the valleys opening out
  Like a volume's turning leaves,

Dreaming of a peak whose height
  Will show me every hill,
A single mountain on whose side
  Life blooms for ever and is still.

KATHLEEN RAINE

The Wilderness

I came too late to the hills: they were swept bare
Winters before I was born of song and story,
Of spell or speech with power of oracle or invocation,

The great ash long dead by a roofless house, its branches rotten,
The voice of the crows an inarticulate cry,
And from the wells and springs the holy water ebbed away.

A child I ran in the wind on a withered moor
Crying out after those great presences who were not there,
Long lost in the forgetfulness of the forgotten.

Only the archaic forms themselves could tell
In sacred speech of hoodie on grey stone, or hawk in air,
Of Eden where the lonely rowan bends over the dark pool.

Yet I have glimpsed the bright mountain behind the mountain,
Knowledge under the leaves, tasted the bitter berries red,
Drunk water cold and clear from an inexhaustible hidden
    fountain.

Sonnet XXIV

Like to these unmeasurable mountains
Is my painful life, the burden of ire:
For of great height be they and high is my desire,
And I of tears and they be full of fountains.
Under craggy rocks they have full barren plains;
Hard thoughts in me my woeful mind doth tire.
Small fruit and many leaves their tops do attire;
Small effect with great trust in me remains.
The boist'rous winds oft their high boughs do blast;
Hot sighs from me continually be shed.
Cattle in them and in me love is fed.
Immovable am I and they are full steadfast.
Of the restless birds they have the tune and note,
And I always plaints that pass thorough my throat.

SAMUEL TAYLOR COLERIDGE

A Stranger Minstrel

As late on Skiddaw's mount I lay supine,
Midway th' ascent, in that repose divine
When the soul centred in the heart's recess
Hath quaff'd its fill of Nature's loveliness,
Yet still beside the fountain's marge will stay
   And fain would thirst again, again to quaff;
Then when the tear, slow travelling on its way,
   Fills up the wrinkles of a silent laugh –
In that sweet mood of sad and humorous thought
A form within me rose, within me wrought
With such strong magic, that I cried aloud,
'Thou ancient Skiddaw by the helm of cloud,
And by thy many-colour'd chasms deep,
And by their shadows that for ever sleep,
By yon small flaky mists that love to creep
Along the edges of those spots of light,
Those sunny islands of thy smooth green height,
   And by yon shepherds with their sheep,
   And dogs and boys, a gladsome crowd,
   That rush e'en now with clamour loud
   Sudden from forth thy topmost cloud,
   And by this laugh, and by this tear,
   I would, old Skiddaw, she were here!
   A lady of sweet song is she,
   Her soft blue eye was made for thee!
   O ancient Skiddaw, by this tear,
   I would, I would that she were here!'

Then ancient Skiddaw, stern and proud,
　In Sullen majesty replying,
Thus spake from out his helm of cloud
　(His voice was like an echo dying!): –
'She dwells belike in scenes more fair,
And scorns a mount so bleak and bare.'

I only sigh'd when this I heard;
Such mournful thoughts within me stirr'd
That all my heart was faint and weak,
　So sorely was I troubled!
No laughter wrinkled on my cheek,
　But O the tears were doubled!
But ancient Skiddaw green and high
Heard and understood my sigh;
And now, in tones less stern and rude,
As if he wish'd to end the feud,
Spake he, the proud response renewing
(His voice was like a monarch wooing): –
'Nay, but thou dost not know her might,
　The pinions of her soul how strong!
But many a stranger in my height
　Hath sung to me her magic song,
　　Sending forth his ecstasy
　　In her divinest melody,
　And hence I know her soul is free,
　She is where'er she wills to be,
　Unfetter'd by mortality!
Now to the 'haunted beach' can fly,
　Beside the threshold scourged with waves,
　Now where the maniac wildly raves,
'Pale moon, thou spectre of the sky!'
　No wind that hurries o'er my height
　Can travel with so swift a flight.
　　I too, methinks, might merit
　　The presence of her spirit!
　　To me too might belong
　The honour of her song and witching melody,
　　Which most resembles me,

Soft, various, and sublime,
Exempt from wrongs of Time!'

Thus spake the mighty Mount, and I
Made answer, with a deep-drawn sigh: –
'Thou ancient Skiddaw, by this tear,
I would, I would that she were here!'

NORMAN NICHOLSON

Scafell Pike

Look
Along the well
Of the street,
Between the gasworks and the neat
Sparrow-stepped gable
Of the Catholic chapel,
High
Above tilt and crook
Of the tumbledown
Roofs of the town –
Scafell Pike,
The tallest hill in England.

How small it seems,
So far away,
No more than a notch
On the plate-glass window of the sky!
Watch
A puff of kitchen smoke
Block out peak and pinnacle –
Rock-pie of volcanic lava
Half a mile thick
Scotched out
At the click of an eye.

Look again
In five hundred, a thousand or ten
Thousand years:
A ruin where
The chapel was; brown
Rubble and scrub and cinders where
The gasworks used to be;
No roofs, no town,

Maybe no men;
But yonder where a lather-rinse of cloud pours down
The spiked wall of the sky-line, see,
Scafell Pike
Still there.

R. S. THOMAS

A Peasant

Iago Prytherch his name, though, be it allowed,
Just an ordinary man of the bald Welsh hills,
Who pens a few sheep in a gap of cloud.
Docking mangels, chipping the green skin
From the yellow bones with a half-witted grin
Of satisfaction, or churning the crude earth
To a stiff sea of clouds that glint in the wind –
So are his days spent, his spittled mirth
Rarer than the sun that cracks the cheeks
Of the gaunt sky perhaps once in a week.
And then at night see him fixed in his chair
Motionless, except when he leans to gob in the fire.
There is something frightening in the vacancy of his mind.
His clothes, sour with years of sweat
And animal contact, shock the refined,
But affected, sense with their stark naturalness.
Yet this is your prototype, who, season by season
Against siege of rain and the wind's attrition,
Preserves his stock, an impregnable fortress
Not to be stormed even in death's confusion.
Remember him, then, for he, too, is a winner of wars,
Enduring like a tree under the curious stars.

EDWARD THOMAS

The Mountain Chapel

Chapel and gravestones, old and few,
Are shrouded by a mountain fold
From sound and view
Of life. The loss of the brook's voice
Falls like a shadow. All they hear is
The eternal noise
Of wind whistling in grass more shrill
Than aught as human as a sword,
And saying still:
''Tis but a moment since man's birth,
And in another moment more
Man lies in earth
For ever; but I am the same
Now, and shall be, even as I was
Before he came:
Till there is nothing I shall be.'

Yet there the sun shines after noon
So cheerfully
The place almost seems peopled, nor
Lacks cottage chimney, cottage hearth:
It is not more
In size than is a cottage, less
Than any other empty home
In homeliness.
It has a garden of wild flowers
And finest grass and gravestones warm
In sunshine hours
The year through. Men behind the glass
Stand once a week, singing, and drown
The whistling grass
Their ponies munch. And yet somewhere
Near or far off there's some man could

Live happy here,
Or one of the gods perhaps, were they
Not of inhuman stature dire
As poets say
Who have not seen them clearly, if
At sound of any wind of the world
In grass-blades stiff
They would not startle and shudder cold
Under the sun. When Gods were young
This wind was old.

The Mountain over Aberdare

From this high quarried ledge I see
The place for which the Quakers once
Collected clothes, my father's home,
Our stubborn bankrupt village sprawled
In jaded dusk beneath its nameless hills;
The drab streets strung across the cwm,
Derelict workings, tips of slag
The gospellers and gamblers use
And children scrutting for the coal
That winter dole cannot purvey;
Allotments where the collier digs
While engines hack the coal within his brain;
Grey Hebron in a rigid cramp,
White cheap-jack cinema, the church
Stretched like a sow beside the stream;
And mourners in their Sunday best
Holding a tiny funeral, singing hymns
That drift insidious as the rain
Which rises from the steaming fields
And swathes about the skyline crags
Till all the upland gorse is drenched
And all the creaking mountain gates
Drip brittle tears of crystal peace;
And in a curtained parlour women hug
Huge grief, and anger against God.

But now the dusk, more charitable than Quakers,
Veils the cracked cottages with drifting may
And rubs the hard day off the slate.
The colliers squatting on the ashtip
Listen to one who holds them still with tales,
While that white frock that floats down the dark alley
Looks just like Christ; and in the lane

The clink of coins among the gamblers
Suggests the thirty pieces of silver.

I watch the clouded years
Rune the rough foreheads of these moody hills,
This wet evening, in a lost age.

ROBERT MINHINNICK

Rhigos

The cannon-smoke rolling
Off the Beacons engulfs the car.
The violence is over
Yet a promise of lightning
With its cordite tang hangs over
The khaki drab of Hirwaun.

Above this mist they gaze
From the stacked flats:
Faces between the turrets,
Hands clenched without weapons.
The only armour here
Is isolation that toughens

The mind, hardens eyes
That stare from siege. I think
Of the people who live
On these battlements: old
Women white and frail as moths,
The men mulattoed by alcohol,

Their frustration which burnt
A hole in life itself burnt out.
Leaving nothing. And as we grind
Over the mountain gridiron
I know they are seeking us
And our movement's illusion

Of freedom, those old people
Standing at their balconies
In the fresh wind, yet
Seeing instead this prow
Of Glamorgan – the black
And naked Rhigos, a whalebacked

Massif that supports
Nothing of their life, that
Is no comfort, yet is the earth
To which they are fused –
Its cloud and violet skeins of light;
An unendurable rock.

EDWARD THOMAS

The Lofty Sky

Today I want the sky,
The tops of the high hills,
Above the last man's house,
His hedges, and his cows,
Where, if I will, I look
Down even on sheep and rook,
And of all things that move
See buzzards only above: –
Past all trees, past furze
And thorn, where naught deters
The desire of the eye
For sky, nothing but sky.
I sicken of the woods
And all the multitudes
Of hedge-trees. They are no more
Than weeds upon this floor
Of the river of air
Leagues deep, leagues wide, where
I am like a fish that lives
In weeds and mud and gives
What's above him no thought.
I might be a tench for aught
That I can do today
Down on the wealden clay.
Even the tench has days
When he floats up and plays
Among the lily leaves
And sees the sky, or grieves
Not if he nothing sees:
While I, I know that trees

Under that lofty sky
Are weeds, fields mud, and I
Would arise and go far
To where the lilies are.

JO SHAPCOTT

Glascwm

This slope has wings, as do our bats
    and the dragonflies and every bird,
        flaunting as if resting on updrafts
    could make a creature invisible.

Look, the light doesn't lie heavy on us
    at all, we can move our legs and arms
        through the honey
                            and even the grass
        wears it worms with grace.

Cefin Hir

Do you see, up there, those high pastures of angels,
        among the heather?
In the strange light
        they seem more than far.

Down the clear valley and right up to the ridge
        you can see yourself break
into fragments which float in the air:
        balloon, bat, RAF Hawk.

Hanter Hill

Tiny rose of light
        a wall crumbling in on itself
the slopes of the hill   or of my cheek
                hesitate

while the excess of light
        stamps its feet
in the lane   all over me
                insisting on the wrong route

TED HUGHES

The Horses

I climbed through woods in the hour-before-dawn dark.
Evil air, a frost-making stillness,

Not a leaf, not a bird –
A world cast in frost. I came out above the wood

Where my breath left tortuous statues in the iron light.
But the valleys were draining the darkness

Till the moorline – blackening dregs of the brightening grey –
Halved the sky ahead. And I saw the horses:

Huge in the dense grey – ten together –
Megalith-still. They breathed, making no move,

With draped manes and tilted hind-hooves,
Making no sound.

I passed: not one snorted or jerked its head.
Grey silent fragments

Of a grey silent world.

I listened in emptiness on the moor-ridge.
The curlew's tear turned its edge on the silence.

Slowly detail leafed from the darkness. Then the sun
Orange, red, red erupted

Silently, and splitting to its core tore and flung cloud,
Shook the gulf open, showed blue,

And the big planets hanging –
I turned

Stumbling in the fever of a dream, down towards
The dark woods, from the kindling tops,

And came to the horses.
                         There, still they stood,
But now steaming and glistening under the flow of light,

Their draped stone manes, their tilted hind-hooves
Stirring under a thaw while all around them

The frost showed its fires. But still they made no sound.
Not one snorted or stamped,

Their hung heads patient as the horizons,
High over valleys, in the red levelling rays –

In din of the crowded streets, going among the years, the faces,
May I still meet my memory in so lonely a place

Between the streams and the red clouds, hearing curlews,
Hearing the horizons endure.

WILLIAM WORDSWORTH

from *The Prelude, Book I*

   Fair seed-time had my soul, and I grew up
Foster'd alike by beauty and by fear;
Much favor'd in my birthplace, and no less
In that beloved Vale to which, erelong,
I was transplanted. Well I call to mind
('Twas at an early age, ere I had seen
Nine summers) when upon the mountain slope
The frost and breath of frosty wind had snapp'd
The last autumnal crocus, 'twas my joy
To wander half the night among the Cliffs
And the smooth Hollows, where the woodcocks ran
Along the open turf. In thought and wish
That time, my shoulder all with springes hung,
I was a fell destroyer. On the heights
Scudding away from snare to snare, I plied
My anxious visitation, hurrying on,
Still hurrying, hurrying onward; moon and stars
Were shining o'er my head; I was alone,
And seem'd to be a trouble to the peace
That was among them. Sometimes it befel
In these night-wanderings, that a strong desire
o'erpower'd my better reason, and the bird
Which was the captive of another's toils
Became my prey; and, when the deed was done
I heard among the solitary hills
Low breathings coming after me, and sounds
Of undistinguishable motion, steps
Almost as silent as the turf they trod.
Nor less in springtime when on southern banks
The shining sun had from his knot of leaves
Decoy'd the primrose flower, and when the Vales
And woods were warm, was I a plunderer then
In the high places, on the lonesome peaks

Where'er, among the mountains and the winds,
The Mother Bird had built her lodge. Though mean
My object, and inglorious, yet the end
Was not ignoble. Oh! when I have hung
Above the raven's nest, by knots of grass
And half-inch fissures in the slippery rock
But ill sustain'd, and almost, as it seem'd,
Suspended by the blast which blew amain,
Shouldering the naked crag; Oh! at that time,
While on the perilous ridge I hung alone,
With what strange utterance did the loud dry wind
Blow through my ears! the sky seem'd not a sky
Of earth, and with what motion mov'd the clouds!

SAMUEL TAYLOR COLERIDGE

from *Reflections on Having Left a Place of Retirement*

Low was our pretty cot: our tallest rose
Peeped at the chamber-window. We could hear
At silent noon, and eve, and early morn,
The sea's faint murmur. In the open air
Our myrtles blossom'd; and across the porch
Thick jasmines twined: the little landscape round
Was green and woody, and refreshed the eye.
It was a spot which you might aptly call
The Valley of Seclusion! Once I saw
(Hallowing his Sabbath-day by quietness)
A wealthy son of commerce saunter by,
Bristowa's citizen: methought, it calmed
His thirst of idle gold, and made him muse
With wiser feelings: for he paused, and looked
With a pleased sadness, and gazed all around,
Then eyed our cottage, and gazed round again,
And sighed, and said, it was a blessed place.
And we *were* blessed. Oft with patient ear
Long-listening to the viewless skylark's note
(Viewless, or haply for a moment seen
Gleaming on sunny wings) in whispered tones
I've said to my beloved, 'Such, sweet girl!
The inobtrusive song of happiness,
Unearthly minstrelsy! then only heard
When the soul seeks to hear; when all is hushed,
And the heart listens!'
                              But the time, when first
From that low dell, steep up the stony mount
I climbed with perilous toil and reached the top,
Oh! what a goodly scene! *Here* the bleak mount,
The bare bleak mountain speckled thin with sheep;

Grey clouds, that shadowing spot the sunny fields;
And river, now with bushy rocks o'erbrowed,
Now winding bright and full, with naked banks;
And seats, and lawns, the abbey and the wood,
And cots, and hamlets, and faint city-spire;
The channel *there*, the islands and white sails,
Dim coasts, and cloudlike hills, and shoreless ocean –
It seemed like Omnipresence! God, methought,
Had built Him there a temple: the whole world
Seemed imaged in its vast circumference,
No *wish* profaned my overwhelmed heart.
Blest hour! It was a luxury, – to be!

'Often rebuked, yet always back returning'

Often rebuked, yet always back returning
  To those first feelings that were born with me,
And leaving busy chase of wealth and learning
  For idle dreams of things which cannot be:

Today, I will seek not the shadowy region;
  Its unsustaining vastness waxes drear;
And visions rising, legion after legion,
  Bring the unreal world too strangely near.

I'll walk, but not in old heroic traces,
  And not in paths of high morality,
And not among the half-distinguished faces,
  The clouded forms of long-past history.

I'll walk where my own nature would be leading:
  It vexes me to choose another guide:
Where the grey flocks in ferny glens are feeding;
  Where the wild wind blows on the mountain side.

What have those lonely mountains worth revealing?
  More glory and more grief than I can tell:
The earth that wakes *one* human heart to feeling
  Can centre both the worlds of Heaven and Hell.

Islands

GEORGE MACKAY BROWN

Hamnavoe

My father passed with his penny letters
Through closes opening and shutting like legends
When barbarous with gulls
Hamnavoe's morning broke

On the salt and tar steps. Herring boats,
Puffing red sails, the tillers
Of cold horizons, leaned
Down the gull-gaunt tide

And threw dark nets on sudden silver harvests.
A stallion at the sweet fountain
Dredged water, and touched
Fire from steel-kissed cobbles.

Hard on noon four bearded merchants
Past the pipe-spitting pier-head strolled,
Holy with greed, chanting
Their slow grave jargon.

A tinker keen like a tartan gull
At cuithe-hung doors. A crofter lass
Trudged through the lavish dung
In a dream of corn-stalks and milk.

In the Arctic Whaler three blue elbows fell,
Regular as waves, from beards spumy with porter,
Till the amber day ebbed out
To its black dregs.

The boats drove furrows homeward, like ploughmen
In blizzards of gulls. Gaelic fisher-girls
Flashed knife and dirge
Over drifts of herring.

And boys with penny wands lured gleams
From tangled veins of the flood. Houses went blind
Up one steep close, for a
Grief by the shrouded nets.

The kirk, in a gale of psalms, went heaving through
A tumult of roofs, freighted for heaven. And lovers
Unblessed by steeples lay under
The buttered bannock of the moon.

He quenched his lantern, leaving the last door.
Because of his gay poverty that kept
My seapink innocence
From the worm and black wind;

And because, under equality's sun,
All things wear now to a common soiling,
In the fire of images
Gladly I put my hand
To save that day for him.

WILLIAM FOWLER

Sonet. In Orknay

Upon the utmost corners of the warld,
and on the borders of this massive round,
quhaire fates and fortoune hither hes me harld,
I doe deplore my greiffs upon this ground;
and seing roring seis from roks rebound
by ebbs and streames of contrair routing tyds,
and phebus chariot in there wawes ly dround,
quha equallye now night and day devyds,
I cal to mynde the storms my thoughts abyds,
which euer wax and never dois decress,
for nights of dole dayes loys ay ever hyds,
and in there vayle doith al my weill suppress:
so this I see, quhaire ever I remove,
I chainge bot sees, but can not chainge my love.

ANONYMOUS

The Great Silkie of Sule Skerry

I am a man, upo da land,
　I am a selkie i da sea;
An whin I'm far fa every strand
　My dwelling is in Shöol Skerry.

An eartly nourris sits and sings,
　And aye she sings, Ba, lily wean!
Little ken I my bairnis father,
　Far less the land that he staps in.

Then ane arose at her bed-fit,
　An a grumly guest I'm sure was he:
'Here am I, thy bairnis father,
　Although that I be not comelie.

'I am a man, upo the lan,
　An I am a silkie in the sea;
And when I'm far and far frae lan,
　My dwelling is in Sule Skerrie.'

'It was na weel,' quo the maiden fair,
　'It was na weel, indeed,' quo she,
'That the Great Silkie of Sule Skerrie
　Suld hae come and aught a bairn to me.'

Now he has taen a purse of goud,
　And he has pat it upo her knee,
Sayin, Gie to me my little young son,
　An tak thee up thy nourris-fee.

An it sall come to pass on a simmer's day,
   When the sin shines het on evera stane,
That I will tak my little young son,
   An teach him for to swim the faem.

An thu sall marry a proud gunner,
   An a proud gunner I'm sure he'll be,
An the very first schot that ere he schoots,
   He'll schoot baith my young son and me.

EDWIN MUIR

The Northern Islands

In favoured summers
These islands have the sun all to themselves
And light a toy to play with, weeks on end.
The empty sky and waters are a shell
Endlessly turning, turning the wheel of light,
While the tranced waves run wavering up the sand.
The beasts sleep when they can, midnight or midday,
Slumbering on into unending brightness.
The green, green fields give too much, are too rank
With beautiful beasts for breeding or for slaughter.
The horses, glorious useless race, are leaving.
Have the old ways left with them, and the faith,
Lost in this dream too comfortable and goodly
To make room for a blessing? Where can it fall?
The old ways change in the turning, turning light,
Taking and giving life to life from life.

JOHN BETJEMAN
Shetland 1973

Fetlar is waiting. At its little quay
  Green seaweed stirs and ripples on the swell.
The lone sham castle looks across at Yell,
And from the mainland hilltops you can see
Over to westward, glimmering distantly,
  The cliffs of Foula as the clouds dispel.
  Clear air, wide skies, crunch underfoot of shell –
The Viking kingdom waits what is to be.

Loud over Lerwick, seabirds wail and squawk,
  Portent of Shetland's fast approaching foes –
The briefcased oilmen with their wily talk;
  Soon we shall see, ranged all along the voes
Their hard-faced wives in ranch-type bungalows.

JEN HADFIELD

Blashey-wadder

At dusk I walked to the postbox,
and the storm that must've passed you earlier today
skirled long, luminous ropes of hail between my feet
and I crackled in my waterproof
like a roasting rack of lamb.

And across the loch,
the waterfalls blew right up off the cliff
in grand plumes like smoking chimneys.

And on the road,
even the puddles ran uphill.

And across Bracadale,
a gritter, as far as I could tell,
rolled a blinking ball of orange light
ahead of it, like a dungbeetle
that had stolen the sun.

And a circlet of iron was torn from a byre
and bowled across the thrift.

And seven wind-whipped cows
clustered under a bluff.

And in a rockpool,
a punctured football reeled around and around.

And even the dog won't heel since yesterday
when – sniffing North addictedly –
he saw we had it coming –

and I mean more'n wet weak hail
on a bastard wind.

LOUIS MACNEICE

The Hebrides

On those islands
The west wind drops its message of indolence,
No one hurries, the Gulf Stream warms the gnarled
Rampart of gneiss, the feet of the peasant years
Pad up and down their sentry-beat not challenging
Any comer for the password – only Death
Comes through unchallenged in his general's cape.
The houses straggle on the umber moors,
The Aladdin lamp mutters in the boarded room
Where a woman smoors the fire of fragrant peat.
No one repeats the password for it is known,
All is known before it comes to the lips –
Instinctive wisdom. Over the fancy vases
The photos with the wrinkles taken out,
The enlarged portraits of the successful sons
Who married wealth in Toronto or New York,
Console the lonely evenings of the old
Who live embanked by memories of labour
And child-bearing and scriptural commentaries.
On those islands
The boys go poaching their ancestral rights –
The Ossianic salmon who take the yellow
Tilt of the river with a magnet's purpose –
And listen breathless to the tales at the ceilidh
Among the peat-smoke and the smells of dung
That fill the felted room from the cave of the byre.
No window opens of the windows sunk like eyes
In a four-foot wall of stones casually picked
From the knuckly hills on which these houses crawl
Like black and legless beasts who breathe in their sleep
Among the piles of peat and pooks of hay –
A brave oasis in the indifferent moors.

And while the stories circulate like smoke,
The sense of life spreads out from the one-eyed house
In wider circles through the lake of night
In which articulate man has dropped a stone –
In wider circles round the black-faced sheep,
Wider and fainter till they hardly crease
The ebony heritage of the herded dead.
On those islands
The tinkers whom no decent girl will go with,
Preserve the Gaelic tunes unspoiled by contact
With the folk-fancier or the friendly tourist,
And preserve the knowledge of horse-flesh and preserve
The uncompromising empire of the rogue.
On those islands
The tethered cow grazes among the orchises
And figures in blue calico turn by hand
The ground beyond the plough, and the bus, not
        stopping,
Drops a parcel for the lonely household
Where men remembering stories of eviction
Are glad to have their land though mainly stones –
The honoured bones which still can hoist a body.
On those islands
There is echo of the leaping fish, the identical
Sound that cheered the chiefs at ease from slaughter;
There is echo of baying hounds of a lost breed
And echo of MacCrimmon's pipes lost in the cave;
And seals cry with the voices of the drowned.
When men go out to fish, no one must say 'Good luck'
And the confidences told in a boat at sea
Must be as if printed on the white ribbon of a wave
Withdrawn as soon as printed – so never heard.
On those islands
The black minister paints the tour of hell
While the unregenerate drink from the bottle's neck
In gulps like gauntlets thrown at the devil's head
And spread their traditional songs across the hills
Like fraying tapestries of fights and loves,

The boar-hunt and the rope let down at night –
Lost causes and lingering home-sickness.
On those islands
The fish come singing from the drunken sea,
The herring rush the gunwales and sort themselves
To cram the expectant barrels of their own accord –
Or such is the dream of the fisherman whose wet
Leggings hang on the door as he sleeps returned
From a night when miles of net were drawn up empty.
On those islands
A girl with candid eyes goes out to marry
An independent tenant of seven acres
Who goes each year to the south to work on the roads
In order to raise a rent of forty shillings,
And all the neighbours celebrate their wedding
With drink and pipes and the walls of the barn reflect
The crazy shadows of the whooping dancers.
On those islands
Where many live on the dole or on old-age pensions
And many waste with consumption and some are
        drowned
And some of the old stumble in the midst of sleep
Into the pot-hole hitherto shunned in dreams
Or falling from the cliff among the shrieks of gulls
Reach the bottom before they have time to wake –
Whoever dies on the islands and however,
The whole of the village goes into three-day mourning,
The afflicted home is honoured and the shops are shut
For on those islands
Where a few surnames cover a host of people
And the art of being a stranger with your neighbour
Has still to be imported, death is still
No lottery ticket in a public lottery –
The result to be read on the front page of a journal –
But a family matter near to the whole family.
On those islands
Where no train runs on rails and the tyrant time
Has no clock-towers to signal people to doom

With semaphore ultimatums tick by tick,
There is still peace though not for me and not
Perhaps for long – still peace on the bevel hills
For those who still can live as their fathers lived
On those islands.

HUGH MACDIARMID

from *Island Funeral*

The procession winds like a little snake
Between the walls of irregular grey stones
Piled carelessly on one another.
Sometimes, on this winding track,
The leaders are doubled back
Quite near to us.

It is a grey world, sea and sky
Are colourless as the grey stones,
And the small fields are hidden by the walls
That fence them on every side.

Seen in perspective, the walls
Overlap each other
As far as the skyline on the hill,
Hiding every blade of grass between them,
So that all the island appears
One jumble of grey boulders.
The last grey wall outlined on the sky
Has the traceried effect
Of a hedge of thorns in winter.

The men in the stiff material
Of their homespun clothes
Look like figures cut from cardboard,
But shod in their rawhide rivelins
They walk with the springing step of mountaineers.
The women wear black shawls,
And black or crimson skirts.

A line of tawny seaweed fringes the bay
Between high-water mark and low.
It is luminous between the grey of rocky shore
And the grey of sullen water.

We can now and then look over a wall
Into some tiny field. Many of these
Are nothing but grey slabs of limestone,
Smooth as any pavement,
With a few blades of grass
Struggling up through the fissures,
And the grey surface of that rock
Catches and holds the light
As if it was water lying there.

At last the long line halts and breaks up,
And, like a stream flowing into a loch,
The crowd pours from the narrow lane
Into the cemetery where on an unfenced sandhill
The grey memorial stones of the island
Have no distinction from the country.
The coffin lies tilted a little sideways
On the dark grey sand flung up from the grave.

A little priest arrives; he has a long body and short legs
And wears bicycle clips on his trousers.
He stands at the head of the grave
And casts a narrow purple ribbon round his neck
And begins without delay to read the Latin prayers
As if they were a string of beads.
Twice the dead woman's son hands him a bottle
And twice he sprinkles the coffin and the grave
With holy water. In all the faces gathered round
There is a strange remoteness.
They are weather-beaten people with eyes grown clear,
Like the eyes of travellers and seamen,
From always watching far horizons.
But there is another legend written on these faces,
A shadow—or a light—of spiritual vision

That will seldom find full play
On the features of country folk
Or men of strenuous action.
Among these mourners are believers and unbelievers,
And many of them steer a middle course,
Being now priest-ridden by convention
And pagan by conviction,
But not one of them betrays a sign
Of facile and self-lulling piety,
Nor can one see on any face
'A sure and certain hope
Of the Resurrection to eternal life.'
This burial is just an act of nature,
A reassertion of the islanders' inborn certainty
That 'in the midst of life we are in death.'
It is unlike the appointed funerals of the mainland
With their bitter pageantry
And the ramp of undertakers and insurance companies
That makes death seem incredible and cruel.
There are no loafing onlookers.
Everyone is immediately concerned
In what is taking place.
All through their lives death has been very close to them,
And this funeral of one who had been 'a grand woman'
Seems to be but a reminder
Of the close comradeship between living and dying.

Down in the bay there is a row of curraghs
Drawn up on the sand. They lie keel upwards,
Each one shining black and smooth
Like some great monster of the sea,
Symbols to the island folk of their age-long
Battle with the waves, a battle where in daily life
The men face death and the women widowhood.

Four men fill in the grave with dark grey sand,
Then they cover the sand
With green sods and rough-hewn boulders,

And finally an old man with a yellow beard
Helps the four young gravediggers
In levering a great slab of stone
Until it lies flat upon the grave,
And the people watch all this in silence.
Then the crowd scatters east and west
And, last, the four gravediggers,
All of them laughing now
With the merriment of clowns.

ANONYMOUS
(translated by K. H. Jackson)

St Columba's Island Hermitage

Delightful I think it to be in the bosom of an isle, on the peak of a rock, that I might often see there the calm of the sea.

That I might see its heavy waves over the glittering ocean, as they chant a melody to their Father on their eternal course.

That I might see its smooth strand of clear headlands, no gloomy thing; that I might hear the voice of the wondrous birds, a joyful tune.

That I might hear the sound of the shallow waves against the rocks; that I might hear the cry by the graveyard, the noise of the sea.

That I might see its splendid flocks of birds over the full-watered ocean; that I might see its mighty whales, greatest of wonders.

That I might see its ebb and its flood-tide in their flow; that this might be my name, a secret I tell, 'He who turned his back on Ireland.'

That contrition of heart should come upon me as I watch it; that I might bewail my many sins, difficult to declare.

That I might bless the Lord who has power over all, Heaven with its pure host of angels, earth, ebb, flood-tide.

That I might pore on one of my books, good for my soul; a while kneeling for beloved Heaven, a while at psalms.

A while gathering dulse from the rock, a while fishing, a while giving food to the poor, a while in my cell.

A while meditating upon the Kingdom of Heaven, holy is the redemption; a while at labour not too heavy; it would be delightful!

DON PATERSON

Luing

When the day comes, as the day surely must,
when is asked of you, and you refuse
to take that lover's wound again, that cup
of emptiness that is our one completion,

I'd say go here, maybe, to our unsung
innermost isle: Kilda's antithesis,
yet still with its own tiny stubborn anthem,
its yellow milkwort and its stunted kye.

Leaving the motherland by a two-car raft,
the littlest of the fleet, you cross the minch
to find yourself, if anything, now deeper
in her arms than ever – sharing her breath,

watching the red vans sliding silently
between her hills. In such intimate exile,
who'd believe the burn behind the house
the straitened ocean written on the map?

Here, beside the fordable Atlantic,
reborn into a secret candidacy,
the fontanelles reopen one by one
in the palms, then the breastbone and the brow,

aching at the shearwater's wail, the rowan
that falls beyond all seasons. One morning
you hover on the threshold, knowing for certain
the first touch of the light will finish you.

KATHLEEN RAINE

Nameless Islets
from *Eireian Chanaiah*

Who dreams these isles,
Image bright in eyes
Of sea-birds circling rocky shores
Where waves beat upon rock, or rock-face smiles
Winter and summer, storm and fair?
In eyes of eider clear under ever-moving ripples the dart
　　and tremor of life;
Bent-grass and wind-dried heather is a curlew's thought,
Gull gazes into being white and shell-strewn sands.

Joy harsh and strange traced in the dawn
A faint and far mirage; to souls archaic and cold
Sun-warmed stones and fish-giving sea were mother stern,
Stone omphalos, birth-caves dark, lost beyond recall.
Home is an image written in the soul,
To each its own: the new-born home to a memory,
Bird-souls, sea-souls, and with them bring anew
The isles that formed the souls, and souls the isles
Are ever building, shell by painted shell
And stone by glittering stone.
The isles are at rest in vision secret and wild,
And high the cliffs in eagle heart exult,
And warm the brown sea-wrack to the seals,
And lichened rocks grey in the buzzard's eye.

ALASTAIR REID

Isle of Arran

Where no one was was where my world was stilled
into hills that hung behind the lasting water,
a quiet quilt of heather where bees slept,
and a single slow bird in circles winding
round the axis of my head.

Any wind being only my breath, the weather
stopped, and a woollen cloud smothered the sun.
Rust and a mist hung over the clock of the day.
A mountain dreamed in the light of the dark
and marsh mallows were yellow for ever.

Still as a fish in the secret loch alone
I was held in the water where my feet found ground
and the air where my head ended,
all thought a prisoner of the still sense –
till a butterfly drunkenly began the world.

To Ailsa Rock

Hearken, thou craggy ocean pyramid!
  Give answer by thy voice, the sea-fowls' screams!
  When were thy shoulders mantled in huge streams?
When from the sun was thy broad forehead hid?
How long is't since the mighty power bid
  Thee heave to airy sleep from fathom dreams?
  Sleep in the lap of thunder or sunbeams,
Or when grey clouds are thy cold coverlid?
Thou answer'st not; for thou art dead asleep.
  Thy life is but two dead eternities –
The last in air, the former in the deep,
  First with the whales, last with the eagle-skies.
Drowned wast thou till an earthquake made thee steep,
  Another cannot wake thy giant size!

NORMAN NICHOLSON

From *Walney Island*

This shore looks back to England: two hundred yards
Of tide, and the boats fratching on their leashes
Like dogs that sniff a stranger. An oily fog
Smudges the mud-mark till the screes of slag
Seem floating on the water. Smoke and fog
Wash over crane and derrick, and chimneystacks
Ripple and ruck in the suck and swim of the air
Like fossil trunks of trees in a drowned forest.
Away in the docks the unlaunched hulls of ships
Seem sunk already, lying on the swash bed
With barnacles and algae.
                              The sea
Flows up the channel, and the insulated eye,
Picking and prodding among old boots and cobbles,
Selects and builds a private landscape – fancy,
Finned like a fish, flashes about an abstract
Underwater world of shapes and shadows,
Where men are only movement, where fire and furnace
Are only highlights, lines and angles. Forms
Lose their function, names soak off the labels,
And upside-down is rightways, while the eye,
Playing at poet with a box of colours,
Daubs its pleasures across the sky.
                              The tide
Turns and slides back, and banks of mud
Heave up like waking sleepers pushing the sheets aside;
And, linking shore to shore, emerges
A dripping rib of concrete, half bridge, half causeway,
With neither curb nor handrail,
A foot above the water. Bare toes or hobnails,
Gripping among the slime and seaweed, find
A short cut to the cockles or to work.
                              And like a stone

Thrown through a window pane, the path
Smashes the panorama, pricking the pattern, bringing back
A human meaning to the scene. Shadows
Are walls again, angles revert to roofs,
And roofs and walls relate themselves to men.
The hunger of a hundred thousand lives
Aches into brick and iron, the pain
Of generations in continual childbirth
Throbs through the squirming smoke, and love and need
Run molten into the cold moulds of time.

JOHN BETJEMAN

A Bay in Anglesey

The sleepy sound of a tea-time tide
Slaps at the rocks the sun has dried,

Too lazy, almost, to sink and lift
Round low peninsulas pink with thrift.

The water, enlarging shells and sand,
Grows greener emerald out from land

And brown over shadowy shelves below
The waving forests of seaweed show.

Here at my feet in the short cliff grass
Are shells, dried bladderwrack, broken glass,

Pale blue squills and yellow rock roses.
The next low ridge that we climb discloses

One more field for the sheep to graze
While, scarcely seen on this hottest of days,

Far to the eastward, over there,
Snowdon rises in pearl-grey air.

Multiple lark-song, whispering bents,
The thymy, turfy and salty scents

And filling in, brimming in, sparkling and free
The sweet susurration of incoming sea.

ROLAND MATHIAS

Porth Cwyfan

June, but the morning's cold, the wind
Bluffing occasional rain. I am clear
What brings me here across the stone
Spit to the island, but not what I shall find
When the dried fribbles of seaweed
Are passed, the black worked into the sandgrains
By the tide's mouthing. I can call nothing my own.

A closed-in, comfortless bay, the branchy
Shifts of voyage everywhere. On a slope
Of sand reaching up to the hidden
Field or stretch of marram, a tipwhite, paunchy
Terrier sits pat on his marker, yapping me
Bodily out of range. What in God's name is he
Guarding that he thinks I want of a sudden?

To the left is the island, granite-hulled
Against froth, the chapel's roof acute
As Cwyfan put it when the finer
Passions ruled, convergent answers belled
Wetherlike towards God. Ahead is the cliff
Eaten by sand. On the quaking field beyond
Low huts, ordered and menacing. Porth China.

Once on the island those last shingle
Feet I came by seem in threat.
Can you, like Beuno, knit me back severed
Heads, Cwyfan, bond men to single
Living? Your nave has a few wild settles
And phantasmagoric dust. And Roger Parry,
Agent to Owen Bold, has a stone skew-whiff in the yard.

Doubling back again is a small
Inevitable tragedy, the umpteenth
In a sinuous month. Now I avoid
The violent pitch of the dog, with all
And nothing to guard, remark his croup,
The hysteric note in the bark. Two dunlin,
Huffing on long legs, pick in and out of the tide.

A man on the beach, a woman
And child with a red woollen cap,
Hummock and stop within earshot,
Eyeing my blundering walk. 'Can
We get to the island?' he asks, Lancashire
Accent humble, dark curls broad. And I
Am suddenly angry. But how is my tripright sounder,
Save that I know Roger Parry and he does not?

CHRISTINE EVANS

Enlli

for Ceri when she was ten

We get to it through troughs and rainbows

flying and falling, falling and flying

rocked in an eggshell
over drowned mountain ranges.

The island swings towards us, slowly.

We slide in on an oiled keel,
step ashore with birth-wet, wind-red faces
wiping the salt from our eyes
and notice sudden, welling
quiet, and how here the breeze
lets smells of growing things
settle and grow warm, a host of presences
drowsing, their wings too fine to see.

There's a green track, lined with meadowsweet.
Stone houses, ramparts to the weather.
Small fields that run all one way
west to the sea, inviting feet
to make new paths to their own
discovered places.

After supper, lamplight
soft as the sheen of buttercups
and candle-shadow blossoms
bold on the bedroom wall.

R. S. THOMAS

Islandmen

And they come sailing
From the island through the flocks
Of the sea with the boat full
Of their own flocks, brimming fleeces
And whelk eyes, with the bleating
Sea-birds and the tide races
Snarling. And the dark hull bites
At the water, crunching it
To small glass, as the men chew
Their tobacco, cleaning their mind
On wind, trusting the horizon's
Logic.
   These are the crusted men
Of the sea, measuring time
By tide-fall, knowing the changeless
Seasons, the lasting honeysuckle
Of the sea. They are lean and hard
And alert, and while our subjects
Increase, burdening us
With their detail, these keep to the one
Fact of the sea, its pitilessness, its beauty.

GWYNETH LEWIS

The Voledom of Skomer

For thirty years a suburban naturalist
has studied the life of the SKOMER VOLE
as a pattern of *rodent parochial*.
His colleagues consider him a purist,
look down on his subject as insular,
but he's entranced by the phenomena of local
and all things SKOMER are his exotica.

He's made a fetish of specificity:
the Ramsey field vole's all very well
and yes, he quite likes the pipistrelle,
but the SKOMER VOLE? – Passionate loyalty
and an endless interest in the ins and outs
of a vole that is wholly residual,
one that missed, as it were, the mainland boat

and, surrounded by water, took a snack and just stayed.
In secret he cherishes a mythic version:
the Ur-Vole, a Moses, leads an excursion
across the causeway on a vole crusade
down the slopes of the slippery Continental Shelf
to Skomer to visionary seclusion,
and the safety of his supernatural self.

In the field he's a hawk-eyed devotee,
finding births, deaths and couplings a revelation,
for one man's life spans many generations
of SKOMER VOLE nations and dynasties.
He stoops like a question while, above him, the sky
tries in vain to touch his imagination;
clouds on their columns of rain pass him by,

for he's not drawn to the world by grandeur
but by hours of waiting for the flash of a tail,
for that blur in the dune grass that might be a male.
No, he's wooed through his voleish sense of wonder,
tied by attention to a piece of land
that he feels, one evening, might just set sail
for its observant and most loving husband.

JOHN DAVIDSON

In the Isle of Dogs

While the water-wagon's ringing showers
Sweetened the dust with a woodland smell,
'Past noon, past noon, two sultry hours,'
Drowsily fell
From the schoolhouse clock
In the Isle of Dogs by Millwall Dock.

Mirrored in shadowy windows draped
With ragged net or half-drawn blind
Bowsprits, masts, exactly shaped
To woo or fight the wind,
Like monitors of guilt
By strength and beauty sent,
Disgraced the shameful houses built
To furnish rent.

From the pavements and the roofs
In shimmering volumes wound
The wrinkled heat;
Distant hammers, wheels and hoofs,
A turbulent pulse of sound,
Southward obscurely beat,
The only utterance of the afternoon,
Till on a sudden in the silent street
An organ-man drew up and ground
The Old Hundredth tune.

Forthwith the pillar of cloud that hides the past
Burst into flame,
Whose alchemy transmuted house and mast,
Street, dockyard, pier and pile:
By magic sound the Isle of Dogs became
A northern isle –
A green isle like a beryl set
In a wine-coloured sea,
Shadowed by mountains where a river met
The ocean's arm extended royally.

There also in the evening on the shore
An old man ground the Old Hundredth tune,
An old enchanter steeped in human lore,
Sad-eyed, with whitening beard, and visage lank:
Not since and not before,
Under the sunset or the mellowing moon,
Has any hand of man's conveyed
Such meaning in the turning of a crank.

Sometimes he played
As if his box had been
An organ in an abbey richly lit;
For when the dark invaded day's demesne,
And the sun set in crimson and in gold;
When idlers swarmed upon the esplanade,
And a late steamer wheeling towards the quay
Struck founts of silver from the darkling sea,
The solemn tune arose and shook and rolled
Above the throng,
Above the hum and tramp and bravely knit
All hearts in common memories of song.

Sometimes he played at speed;
Then the Old Hundredth like a devil's mass
Instinct with evil thought and evil deed,
Rang out in anguish and remorse. Alas!
That men must know both Heaven and Hell!
Sometimes the melody
Sang with the murmuring surge;
And with the winds would tell
Of peaceful graves and of the passing bell.
Sometimes it pealed across the bay
A high triumphal dirge,
A dirge
For the departing undefeated day.

A noble tune, a high becoming mate
Of the capped mountains and the deep broad firth;
A simple tune and great,
The fittest utterance of the voice of earth.

POLLY CLARK

Fishing Boat

I wanted so much to save it,
the carved sea, the white sky
bleaching me away.

The peregrines whipped from the chalk,
rushed up the cliff-face
like ash from the baking sea,

and I wanted so much to save it,
how we lay down, and the sun
fired our shadows into the rock.

Far below a fishing boat chugged
like a toy, pushing its blue V
to somewhere familiar.

And I saw the skipper recording,
I saw that he would be the one
to draft the flutter of clothes,

the obliteration of skin by sun,
the *are they . . . ? are they . . . ?*
as the boat led him out of sight

of the dust and pebbles kicked
slowly down the chalky face.
I saw him scribbling the whispers,

the madness, the too-little time,
as the boat and its trawl of glimpses
slipped away from me, towards home.

ANONYMOUS

(translated by Michael Alexander)

Wulf and Eadwacer

The men of my tribe would treat him as game:
if he comes to the camp they will kill him outright.

    Our fate is forked.

Wulf is on one island, I on another.
Mine is a fastness: the fens girdle it
and it is defended by the fiercest men.
If he comes to the camp they will kill him for sure.

    Our fate is forked.

It was rainy weather, and I wept by the hearth,
thinking of my Wulf's far wanderings;
one of the captains caught me in his arms.
It gladdened me then; but it grieved me too.

Wulf, my Wulf, it was wanting you
that made me sick, your seldom coming,
the hollowness at heart; not the hunger I spoke of.

Do you hear, Eadwacer? Our whelp
    Wulf shall take to the wood.
What was never bound is broken easily,
    our song together.

from *The Battle of Maldon*

Bryhtnoth spoke. He raised shield-board,
shook the slim ash-spear, shaped his words.
Stiff with anger, he gave him answer:

'Hearest 'ou, seaman, what this folk sayeth?
Spears shall be all the tribute they send you,
viper-stained spears and the swords of forebears,
such a haul of harness as shall hardly profit you.

Spokesman for scavengers, go speak this back again,
bear your tribe a bitterer tale:
that there stands here 'mid his men not the meanest of Earls,
pledged to fight in this land's defence,
the land of Aethelred, my liege lord,
its soil, its folk. In this fight the heathen
shall fall. It would be a shame for your trouble
if you should with our silver away to ship
without fight offered. It is a fair step hither:
you have come a long way into our land.

But English silver is not so softly won:
first iron and edge shall make arbitrament,
harsh war-trial, ere we yield tribute.'

He bade his brave men bear their shields forward
until they all stood at the stream's edge,
though they might not clash yet for the cleaving waters.
After the ebb the flood came flowing in;
the sea's arms locked. Overlong it seemed
before they might bear spear-shafts in shock together.

So they stood by Panta's stream in proud array,
the ranks of the East Saxons and the host from the ash-ships,
nor might any of them harm another
save who through arrow-flight fell dead.

The flood went out. Eager the fleet-men stood,
the crowding raiders, ravening for battle;
then the heroes' Helm bade hold the causeway
a war-hard warrior – Wulfstan was his name –
come of brave kin. It was this Ceola's son
who with his Frankish spear struck down the first man there
as he so boldly stepped onto the bridge's stonework.

There stood with Wulfstan staunch warriors,
Aelfere and Maccus, men of spirit
who would not take flight from the ford's neck
but fast defence make against the foemen
the while that they might wield their weapons.
When the hated strangers saw and understood
what bitter bridge-warders were brought against them there,
they began to plead with craft, craving leave
to fare over the ford and lead across their footmen.

Then the Earl was overswayed by his heart's arrogance
to allow overmuch land to that loath nation:
the men stood silent as Brighthelm's son
called out over the cold water.

   'The ground is cleared for you: come quickly to us,
   gather to battle. God alone knows
   who shall carry the wielding of this waste ground.'

The war-wolves waded across, mourned not for the water,
the Viking warrior-band; came west over Pant,
bearing shield-boards over sheer water
and up onto land, lindenwood braced.

Against their wrath there stood in readiness
Bryhtnoth amid his band. He bade them work
the war-hedge with their targes, and the troop to stand
fast against foe. Then neared the fight,
the glory-trial. The time grew on
when there the fated men must fall;
the war-cry was raised up. Ravens wound higher,
the eagle, carrion-eager; on earth – the cry!

Out flashed file-hard point from fist,
sharp-ground spears sprang forth,
bows were busy, bucklers flinched,
it was a bitter battle-clash. On both halves
brave men fell, boys lay still.

It was then that Wulfmaer was wounded, war-rest chose,
Bryhtnoth's kinsman; he was beaten down,
his sister's son, under the swords' flailing.
But straight wreaking requital on the Vikings,
Edward (as I heard) so struck one man
– the sword-arm stiff, not stinting the blow –
that the fated warrior fell at his feet:
deed for which Bryhtnoth, when a breathing space came,
spoke his thanks to his bower-thane.

So they stood fast, those stout-hearted
warriors at the war-play, watching fiercely
who there with spear might first dispatch
a doomed man's life. The dying fell to earth;
others stood steadfast. Bryhtnoth stirred them,
bade every man there turn mood to deeds
who would that day's doom wrest from out the Danish ranks.

Bryhtnoth war-hard braced shield-board,
shook out his sword, strode firmly
towards his enemy, earl to churl,
in either's heart harm to the other.

T. S. ELIOT

Defence of the Islands

Let these memorials of built stone—music's
enduring instrument, of many centuries of
patient cultivation of the earth, of English
verse

be joined with the memory of this defence of
the islands

and the memory of those appointed to the grey
ships—battleship, merchantman, trawler—
contributing their share to the ages' pavement
of British bone on the sea floor

and of those who, in man's newest form of gamble
with death, fight the power of darkness in air
and fire

and of those who have followed their forebears
to Flanders and France, those undefeated in de-
feat, unalterable in triumph, changing nothing
of their ancestors' ways but the weapons

and those again for whom the paths of glory are
the lanes and the streets of Britain:

to say, to the past and the future generations
of our kin and of our speech, that we took up
our positions, in obedience to instructions.

WILLIAM SHAKESPEARE

from *Richard II, Act 2, Scene 1*

This royal throne of kings, this scepter'd isle,
This earth of majesty, this seat of Mars,
This other Eden, demi-paradise,
This fortress built by Nature for herself
Against infection and the hand of war,
This happy breed of men, this little world,
This precious stone set in the silver sea,
Which serves it in the office of a wall,
Or as a moat defensive to a house,
Against the envy of less happier lands,
This blessed plot, this earth, this realm, this England,
This nurse, this teeming womb of royal kings,
Fear'd by their breed and famous by their birth,
Renowned for their deeds as far from home, –
For Christian service and true chivalry, –
As is the sepulchre in stubborn Jewry
Of the world's ransom, blessed Mary's Son:
This land of such dear souls, this dear, dear land,
Dear for her reputation through the world,
Is now leas'd out, – I die pronouncing it, –
Like to a tenement, or pelting farm:
England, bound in with the triumphant sea,
Whose rocky shore beats back the envious siege
Of watery Neptune, is now bound in with shame,
With inky blots, and rotten parchment bonds:
That England, that was wont to conquer others,
Hath made a shameful conquest of itself.

On This Island

Look, stranger, on this island now
The leaping light for your delight discovers,
Stand stable here
And silent be,
That through the channels of the ear
May wander like a river
The swaying sound of the sea.

Here at the small field's ending pause
When the chalk wall falls to the foam and its tall ledges
Oppose the pluck
And knock of the tide,
And the shingle scrambles after the sucking surf,
And the gull lodges
A moment on its sheer side.

Far off like floating seeds the ships
Diverge on urgent voluntary errands,
And the full view
Indeed may enter
And move in memory as now these clouds do,
That pass the harbour mirror
And all the summer through the water saunter.

RUARAIDH MACTHÒMAIS/ DERICK THOMSON

The Second Island

When we reached the island
it was evening
and we were at peace,
the sun lying down
under the sea's quilt
and the dream beginning anew.

But in the morning
we tossed the cover aside
and in that white light
saw a loch in the island,
and an island in the loch,
and we recognised
that the dream had moved away from us again.

The stepping-stones are chancy
to the second island,
the stone totters
that guards the berries,
the rowan withers,
we have lost now the scent of the honeysuckle.

Woods and Forests

LOUIS MACNEICE

Woods

My father who found the English landscape tame
Had hardly in his life walked in a wood,
Too old when first he met one; Malory's knights,
Keats's nymphs or the Midsummer Night's Dream
Could never arras the room, where he spelled out True and Good
With their interleaving of half-truths and not-quites.

While for me from the age of ten the socketed wooden gate
Into a Dorset planting, into a dark
But gentle ambush, was an alluring eye;
Within was a kingdom free from time and sky,
Caterpillar webs on the forehead, danger under the feet,
And the mind adrift in a floating and rustling ark

Packed with birds and ghosts, two of every race,
Trills of love from the picture-book – Oh might I never land
But here, grown six foot tall, find me also a love
Also out of the picture-book; whose hand
Would be soft as the webs of the wood and on her face
The wood-pigeon's voice would shaft a chrism from above.

So in a grassy ride a rain-filled hoof-mark coined
By a finger of sun from the mint of Long Ago
Was the last of Lancelot's glitter. Make-believe dies hard;
That the rider passed here lately and is a man we know
Is still untrue, the gate to Legend remains unbarred,
The grown-up hates to divorce what the child joined.

Thus from a city when my father would frame
Escape, he thought, as I do, of bog or rock
But I have also this other, this English, choice
Into what yet is foreign; whatever its name
Each wood is the mystery and the recurring shock
Of its dark coolness is a foreign voice.

Yet in using the word tame my father was maybe right,
These woods are not the Forest; each is moored
To a village somewhere near. If not of today
They are not like the wilds of Mayo, they are assured
Of their place by men; reprieved from the neolithic night
By gamekeepers or by Herrick's girls at play.

And always we walk out again. The patch
Of sky at the end of the path grows and discloses
An ordered open air long ruled by dyke and fence,
With geese whose form and gait proclaim their consequence,
Pargetted outposts, windows browed with thatch,
And cow pats – and inconsequent wild roses.

WILLIAM SHAKESPEARE

from *As You Like It, Act 2, Scene 1*

Are not these woods
More free from peril than the envious court?
Here feel we but the penalty of Adam,
The seasons' difference; as, the icy fang
And churlish chiding of the winter's wind,
Which, when it bites and blows upon my body,
Even till I shrink with cold, I smile and say
'This is no flattery: these are counsellors
That feelingly persuade me what I am.'
Sweet are the uses of adversity,
Which like the toad, ugly and venomous,
Wears yet a precious jewel in his head;
And this our life exempt from public haunt,
Finds tongues in trees, books in the running brooks,
Sermons in stones, and good in every thing.
I would not change it.

CHRISTINA ROSSETTI

The Trees' Counselling.

I was strolling sorrowfully
    Thro' the corn fields and the meadows;
The stream sounded melancholy,
    And I walked among the shadows;
While the ancient forest trees
Talked together in the breeze;
In the breeze that waved and blew them,
With a strange weird rustle thro' them.

Said the oak unto the others
    In a leafy voice and pleasant:
'Here we all are equal brothers,
    'Here we have nor lord nor peasant.
'Summer, Autumn, Winter, Spring,
'Pass in happy following.
'Little winds may whistle by us,
'Little birds may overfly us;

'But the sun still waits in heaven
    'To look down on us in splendour;
'When he goes the moon is given,
    'Full of rays that he doth lend her:
'And tho' sometimes in the night
'Mists may hide her from our sight,
'She comes out in the calm weather,
'With the glorious stars together.'

From the fruitage, from the blossom,
    From the trees came no denying;
Then my heart said in my bosom:
    'Wherefore art thou sad and sighing?
'Learn contentment from this wood
'That proclaimeth all states good;

'Go not from it as it found thee;
'Turn thyself and gaze around thee.'

And I turned: behold the shading
   But showed forth the light more clearly;
The wild bees were honey-lading;
   The stream sounded hushing merely,
And the wind not murmuring
Seemed, but gently whispering:
'Get thee patience; and thy spirit
'Shall discern in all things merit.'

BRIAN PATTEN

A Talk with a Wood

Moving through you one evening
when you offered shelter to
quiet things soaked in rain

I saw through your thinning branches
the beginnings of suburbs, and
frightened by the rain,

grey hares running upright in
distant fields; and quite alone there
I thought of nothing but my footprints

being filled, and love, distilled
of people, drifted free, then
the woods spoke with me.

ANDREW MARVELL

The Garden

How vainly men themselves amaze
To win the Palm, the Oke, or Bayes;
And their uncessant Labours see
Crown'd from some single Herb or Tree,
Whose short and narrow vergéd shade
Does prudently their Toyles upbraid;
While all Flow'rs and all Trees do close
To weave the Garlands of repose.

Fair quiet, have I found thee here,
And Innocence thy Sister dear!
Mistaken long, I sought you then
In busie Companies of Men:
Your sacred Plants, if here below,
Only among the Plants will grow;
Society is all but rude,
To this delicious Solitude.

No white nor red was ever seen
So am'rous as this lovely green.
Fond Lovers, cruel as their Flame,
Cut in these Trees their Mistress' name.
Little, Alas, they know, or heed,
How far these Beauties Hers exceed!
Fair Trees! where se'er your barks I wound
No Name shall but your own be found.

When we have run our Passions heat,
Love hither makes his best retreat.
The gods that mortal Beauty chase,
Still in a Tree did end their race.
Apollo hunted *Daphne* so,
Only that She might Laurel grow.

And *Pan* did after *Syrinx* speed,
Not as a Nymph, but for a Reed.

What wond'rous Life is this I lead!
Ripe Apples drop about my head;
The Luscious Clusters of the Vine
Upon my Mouth do crush their Wine;
The Nectaren, and curious Peach,
Into my hands themselves do reach;
Stumbling on Melons, as I pass,
Insnar'd with Flow'rs, I fall on Grass.

Mean while the Mind, from pleasure less,
Withdraws into its happiness:
The Mind, that Ocean where each kind
Does streight its own resemblance find;
Yet it creates, transcending these,
Far other Worlds, and other Seas;
Annihilating all that's made
To a green Thought in a green Shade.

Here at the fountain's sliding foot,
Or at some Fruit-trees mossy root,
Casting the Bodies Vest aside,
My Soul into the boughs does glide:
There like a Bird it sits, and sings,
Then whets, and combs its silver Wings;
And, till prepar'd for longer flight,
Waves in its Plumes the various Light.

Such was that happy Garden-state,
While Man there walk'd without a Mate:
After a Place so pure and sweet,
What other Help could yet be meet!
But 'twas beyond a Mortal's share
To wander solitary there:
Two Paradises 'twere in one
To live in Paradise alone.

How well the skilful Gardner drew
Of flow'rs and herbes this Dial new;
Where from above the milder Sun
Does through a fragrant Zodiack run;
And, as it works, th' industrious Bee
Computes its time as well as we.
How could such sweet and wholesome Hours
Be reckon'd but with herbs and flow'rs!

EDWARD, LORD HERBERT OF CHERBURY

Sonnet: On the Groves Near Merlou Castle

You well-compacted groves, whose light and shade
    Mixed equally produce nor heat nor cold,
    Either to burn the young, or freeze the old,
But to one even temper being made,
Upon a green embroidering through each glade
    An airy silver, and a sunny gold,
    So clothe the poorest that they do behold
Themselves in riches which can never fade,
    While the wind whistles, and the birds do sing,
While your twigs clip, and while your leaves do kiss,
    While the fruit ripens which those trunks do bring,
    Senseless to all but love, do you not spring
Pleasure of such a kind, as truly is
A self-renewing vegetable bliss?

SIEGFRIED SASSOON

Wind in the Beechwood

The glorying forest shakes and swings with glancing
Of boughs that dip and strain; young, slanting sprays
Beckon and shift like lissom creatures dancing,
While the blown beechwood streams with drifting rays.
   Rooted in steadfast calm, grey stems are seen
   Like weather-beaten masts; the wood, unfurled,
   Seems as a ship with crowding sails of green
   That sweeps across the lonely billowing world.

O luminous and lovely! Let your flowers,
Your ageless-squadroned wings, your surge and gleam,
Drown me in quivering brightness: let me fade
   In the warm, rustling music of the hours
   That guard your ancient wisdom, till my dream
   Moves with the chant and whisper of the glade.

EDWARD THOMAS

Aspens

All day and night, save winter, every weather,
Above the inn, the smithy, and the shop,
The aspens at the cross-roads talk together
Of rain, until their last leaves fall from the top.

Out of the blacksmith's cavern comes the ringing
Of hammer, shoe, and anvil; out of the inn
The clink, the hum, the roar, the random singing –
The sounds that for these fifty years have been.

The whisper of the aspens is not drowned,
And over lightless pane and footless road,
Empty as sky, with every other sound
Not ceasing, calls their ghosts from their abode,

A silent smithy, a silent inn, nor fails
In the bare moonlight or the thick-furred gloom,
In tempest or the night of nightingales,
To turn the cross-roads to a ghostly room.

And it would be the same were no house near.
Over all sorts of weather, men, and times,
Aspens must shake their leaves and men may hear
But need not listen, more than to my rhymes.

Whatever wind blows, while they and I have leaves
We cannot other than an aspen be
That ceaselessly, unreasonably grieves,
Or so men think who like a different tree.

ROBERT FROST

The Sound of the Trees

I wonder about the trees.
Why do we wish to bear
Forever the noise of these
More than another noise
So close to our dwelling place?
We suffer them by the day
Till we lose all measure of pace,
And fixity in our joys,
And acquire a listening air.
They are that that talks of going
But never gets away;
And that talks no less for knowing,
As it grows wiser and older,
That now it means to stay.
My feet tug at the floor
And my head sways to my shoulder
Sometimes when I watch trees sway,
From the window or the door.
I shall set forth for somewhere,
I shall make the reckless choice
Some day when they are in voice
And tossing so as to scare
The white clouds over them on.
I shall have less to say,
But I shall be gone.

LLYWELYN AP Y MOEL
(translated by Tony Conran)

To the Greyrock Woods

By God, you're a fine Wood, hillock
Of Grey slate, Llech Ysgar Rock,
Circle of leaf, Irish snare –
God's grace along your verdure!
Row on row, you're clustered round
A fort, a warrior's playground,
A bracken glade, a snug lair –
How strange would be the summer
(Love's herald, I would argue)
If I were left without you
Where the weft of your twigs knits
Your hills, your leafy turrets!
You're my lord, my heaven gate,
My honour saved, my helpmate,
My saint and my true warrant,
My great house, my settlement.
Faultless nurture, it's been good
To have you for my safeguard,
Sweet close and veil of refuge,
Strong and swiftly sheltering hedge,
Beneath me level greensward,
Green, kind earth, gem of a lord,
Trusses of sweet leaves crowded
Like a dark tent overhead:
My bed is snug in safety,
Your branches overhead me
Are no turf-topped villein's den –
Fine, with the porridge eaten!
Better than bardic travel
For one anxious to do well
Is to strip a Saxon's harness
Off him in this pleasant place,

To scare with din and mischief,
And (you teach us) to break leaf
And hear from a fair castle,
In pure tune, the nightingale.
They've trailed me round the hilltop
Many a tie; you give me hope
On snow ways, dark and trackless,
Where at night no English pass.

Wide circle above our den,
To Owain's men you're London.
Meanwhile, England's state is marred –
God grant our fight goes forward!
To our side all good fortune,
All reward to Owain's men!

ANONYMOUS

(translated by Bernard O'Donahue)

from *Sir Gawain and the Green Knight*

'By Our Lady,' said the guide, 'since what you say means
you want to bring destruction down on yourself
and lose your life, who am I to stop you?
Here, take your helmet, grasp your spear in your hand
and ride down this track by the side of the rock
till you come to the depths of that wide valley.
Then look a bit to the side, to your left hand,
and you'll see in the clearing the chapel itself
and the burly warrior that holds it by force.
Now farewell in God's name, noble Sir Gawain!
For all the wealth of the world I wouldn't go with you
nor stay in your company another foot through this forest.'
Whereupon, in the wood he turned his reins,
spurred on his horse as hard as he could
and galloped away, leaving the knight
        all on his own.
        'By God Himself,' said Gawain,
        'I'll neither weep nor wail.
        To God's will I am bound
        and dedicated to Him.'

Then he spurred on Gryngolet and picked up the path,
pressed on past a rock at the edge of a copse
and rode down the rough slope right to the depths.
There he looked around and saw how wild it all was,
with no sign of a refuge anywhere:
just high and steep banks, and on every side
rough gnarled crags and knuckled stones.
The clouds seemed to him to be grazed by the rocks.
He stopped and reined in his horse for a while,
looking in all directions to find the Green Chapel.
He saw nothing of the kind, which struck him as strange,

except, a little way off, a kind of a hump:
a rounded mound on the hill by the water,
near the bed of a stream that ran by there.
The water seethed in it as if it was boiling.
The knight spurred his horse and rode up to the mound,
jumped down nimbly and fastened the reins
of his fine steed to the branch of a lime tree.
Then he turned to the barrow and walked all round it,
pondering with himself what on earth it might be.
It had a hole at the end and on either side,
and was covered all over with clumps of grass.
It was hollow inside, just some old cave
or a gap in an old crag. He couldn't describe it
      in words.
      'Well, Lord,' said the knight.
      'Can this be the Green Chapel?
      A place fit for the Devil
      to say morning prayers at night.'

'Certainly,' said Gawain, 'it's desolate round here,
an ugly oratory indeed, overgrown with weeds.
It's well suited for that knight in green
to offer up his prayers to the Devil.
I'm beginning to suspect, by all my five senses,
that it's Him who has brought me here for destruction.
It is a chapel of doom, bad luck to it!
It's the damnedest church I've ever been in!'
With his helmet on and his lance at the ready,
he climbed up to the roof of that structure.
Then he heard from a huge rock on the hillside,
from the slope across the stream, a deafening noise.
Listen! It clattered on the cliff as if it would split it,
like someone edging a scythe on a stone.
Listen! It whirred and ground like water in a mill-race;
it rushed and rang, terrifying to hear.
'God!' said Gawain, 'this reception, I fancy,
is prepared in my honour, to celebrate me
      properly.
      God's will be done! "Alas!"'ing

will do no good.
Though I'm to lose my life,
no noise will make me tremble.'

Then the knight called out very loudly:
'Who's in charge of this place, to keep my appointment?
For now faithful Gawain is standing here.
If anyone wants something, let him come out at once,
now or never, and make his demand.'
'Hold on,' said someone straight over his head,
'and you will receive all I once promised you.'
He went on making that noise for a while,
turning back to his sharpening before he'd come down.
Then he appeared by a crag, coming out of a crevice,
striding from a gap with a desperate weapon,
a Danish axe ready to deliver the blow,
with its huge blade arching back to the shaft,
filed on the grindstone, four feet long.
It was that long, measured by its tassel.
And, as before, the man was all green –
face and legs, hair and beard –
except that now he travelled on foot,
planking the handle on the rock and striding along.
When he got to the water, not wanting to wade,
he vaulted over on his axe and strode aggressively
with grim purpose across that wide field,
            covered with snow.
        Sir Gawain met the knight
        without bowing too low.
        The knight said, 'Good Sir,
        you're a man who keeps his word.'

EDMUND SPENSER

from *The Faerie Queene, Book 6*

Unto this place when as the Elfin Knight
  Approcht, him seemed that the merry sound
  Of a shrill pipe he playing heard on hight,
  And many feete fast thumping th'hollow ground,
  That through the woods their Eccho did rebound.
  He nigher drew, to weete what mote it be;
  There he a troupe of Ladies dauncing found
  Full merrily, and making gladfull glee,
And in the midst a Shepheard piping he did see.

He durst not enter into th'open greene,
  For dread of them unwares to be descryde,
  For breaking of their daunce, if he were seene;
  But in the covert of the wood did byde,
  Beholding all, yet of them unespyde.
  There he did see, that pleased much his sight,
  That even he him selfe his eyes envyde,
  An hundred naked maidens lilly white,
All raunged in a ring, and dauncing in delight.

SIR THOMAS WYATT
Song CCLXI

I must go walk the woods so wild
   And wander here and there
   In dread and deadly fear,
For where I trust, I am beguiled
   And all for your love, my dear.

I am banished from my bliss
   By craft and false pretence,
   Faultless, without offence;
And of return no certain is
   And all for your love, my dear.

Banished am I, remediless,
   To wilderness alone,
   Alone to sigh and moan
And of relief all comfortless
   And all for your love, my dear.

My house shall be the greenwood tree,
   A tuft of brakes my bed.
   And this my life I lead
As one that from his joy doth flee
   And all for your love, my dear.

The running streams shall be my drink.
   Acorns shall be my food.
   Naught else shall do me good
But on your beauty for to think
   And all for your love, my dear.

And when the deer draw to the green,
  Makes me think on a roe:
  How I have seen ye go
Above the fairest, fairest beseen!
  And all for your love, my dear.

But where I see in any coast
  Two turtles sit and play,
  Rejoicing all the day,
Alas, I think, this have I lost
  And all for your love, my dear.

No bird, no bush, no bough I see
  But bringeth to my mind
  Something whereby I find
My heart far wandered, far fro me,
  And all for your love, my dear.

The tune of birds when I do hear,
  My heart doth bleed, alas,
  Remembering how I was
Wont for to hear your ways so clear
  And all for your love, my dear.

My thought doth please me for the while:
  While I see my desire
  Naught else I do require.
So with my thought I me beguile
  And all for your love, my dear.

Yet I am further from my thought
  Than earth from heaven above.
  And yet for to remove
My pain, alas, availeth naught
  And all for your love, my dear.

LADY MARY WROTH

from *Pamphilia to Amphilanthus*

Late in the Forest I did Cupid see
    colde, wett, and crying hee had lost his way,
    and beeing blind was farder like to stray:
    which sight a kind compassion bred in mee,

I kindly tooke, and dride him, while that hee
    poore child complain'd hee sterved was with stay,
    and pin'de for want of his accustom'd pray,
    for non in that wilde place his hoste would bee,

I glad was of his finding, thinking sure
    this service should my freedome still procure,
    and in my armes I tooke him then unharmde,

Carrying him safe unto a Mirtle bowre
    butt in the way hee made mee feele his powre,
    burning my hart who had him kindly warmd.

THOMAS HARDY

In a Wood

Pale beech and pine so blue,
　　　Set in one clay,
Bough to bough cannot you
　　　Live out your day?
When the rains skim and skip,
Why mar sweet comradeship,
Blighting with poison-drip
　　　Neighbourly spray?

Heart-halt and spirit-lame,
　　　City-opprest,
Unto this wood I came
　　　As to a nest;
Dreaming that sylvan peace
Offered the harrowed ease –
Nature a soft release
　　　From men's unrest.

But, having entered in,
　　　Great growths and small
Show them to men akin –
　　　Combatants all
Sycamore shoulders oak,
Bines the slim sapling yoke,
Ivy-spun halters choke
　　　Elms stout and tall.

Touches from ash, O wych,
        Sting you like scorn!
You, too, brave hollies, twitch
        Sidelong from thorn.
Even the rank poplars bear
Lothly a rival's air,
Cankering in black despair
        If overborne.

Since, then, no grace I find
        Taught me of trees,
Turn I back to my kind,
        Worthy as these.
There at least smiles abound,
There discourse trills around,
There, now and then, are found
        Life-loyalties.

GWYNETH LEWIS

Woods

Midwinter and this beech wood's mind
is somewhere else. Like fallen light

snow's broken glass fills up the furrows.
Nothing that doesn't have to moves.

We walk through a frozen waterfall
of boles, all held in vertical

except for the careful woodpile laid
in pencils across a tidied glade.

Look back and from the place we were
a bird calls out because we're not there,

a double note whose range expands,
pushing the line where our racket ends

out ever further. That elaborate song
can only exist because we're gone.

A vandal, I shatter that place with a stone.
The bird is for silence. I am for home.

ANNE BRONTË

The Arbour

I'll rest me in this sheltered bower,
And look upon the clear blue sky
That smiles upon me through the trees,
Which stand so thickly clustering by;

And view their green and glossy leaves,
All glistening in the sunshine fair;
And list the rustling of their boughs,
So softly whispering through the air.

And while my ear drinks in the sound,
My winged soul shall fly away;
Reviewing long departed years
As one mild, beaming, autumn day;

And soaring on to future scenes,
Like hills and woods, and valleys green,
All basking in the summer's sun,
But distant still, and dimly seen.

Oh, list! 'tis summer's very breath
That gently shakes the rustling trees –
But look! the snow is on the ground –
How can I think of scenes like these?

'Tis but the *frost* that clears the air,
And gives the sky that lovely blue;
They're smiling in a *winter's* sun,
Those evergreens of sombre hue.

And winter's chill is on my heart –
How can I dream of future bliss?
How can my spirit soar away,
Confined by such a chain as this?

CRAIG RAINE

In the Woods

Always at this time there is the bankrupt plant:
autumn afflicts the failed machinery of ferns with rust.
The foliage is full of broken windows.
The birch trees shed their aluminium crust,

and the cedar drops its complicated cogs.
The roof of things has fallen in –
these paprika patches on the factory floor
are corrugated remnants of protective tin.

Oddments blacken strangely on a nearby fence:
rags, an old glove in a liquorice droop,
washleathers warp with dull black holly claws.
It is a sad, abandoned, oddly human group.

The glove is singular. You cannot try it on.
It is too small. Besides, it has no fingers.
It is more like something surgical –
the unpleasant shape of stumpy enigmas.

Below, a nylon sock curls up like a dead animal.
Through a hole in the toe, a glint of teeth.
Over there, the remains of a fire –
pigeon feathers in a narrow ashy wreath.

And everywhere egg-shells, egg-shells,
so light they stir with the gentlest breath –
a breakfast of papery skulls. The Omelette Man
has eaten here and manufactured death.

TED HUGHES

Hawk Roosting

I sit in the top of the wood, my eyes closed.
Inaction, no falsifying dream
Between my hooked head and hooked feet:
Or in sleep rehearse perfect kills and eat.

The convenience of the high trees!
The air's buoyancy and the sun's ray
Are of advantage to me;
And the earth's face upward for my inspection.

My feet are locked upon the rough bark.
It took the whole of Creation
To produce my foot, my each feather:
Now I hold Creation in my foot

Or fly up, and revolve it all slowly –
I kill where I please because it is all mine.
There is no sophistry in my body:
My manners are tearing off heads –

The allotment of death.
For the one path of my flight is direct
Through the bones of the living.
No arguments assert my right:

The sun is behind me.
Nothing has changed since I began.
My eye has permitted no change.
I am going to keep things like this.

THOMAS HARDY

The Darkling Thrush

I leant upon a coppice gate
    When Frost was spectre-grey,
And Winter's dregs made desolate
    The weakening eye of day.
The tangled bine-stems scored the sky
    Like strings of broken lyres,
And all mankind that haunted nigh
    Had sought their household fires.

The land's sharp features seemed to be
    The Century's corpse outleant,
His crypt the cloudy canopy,
    The wind his death-lament.
The ancient pulse of germ and birth
    Was shrunken hard and dry,
And every spirit upon earth
    Seemed fervourless as I.

At once a voice arose among
    The bleak twigs overhead
In a full-hearted evensong
    Of joy illimited;
An aged thrush, frail, gaunt, and small,
    In blast-beruffled plume,
Had chosen thus to fling his soul
    Upon the growing gloom.

So little cause for carolings
    Of such ecstatic sound
Was written on terrestrial things
    Afar or nigh around,
That I could think there trembled through
    His happy good-night air
Some blessed Hope, whereof he knew
    And I was unaware.

GERARD MANLEY HOPKINS

Spring and Fall
To a Young Child

Márgarét, áre you gríeving
Over Goldengrove unleaving?
Leáves, líke the things of man, you
With your fresh thoughts care for, can you?
Áh! ás the heart grows older
It will come to such sights colder
By and by, nor spare a sigh
Though worlds of wanwood leafmeal lie;
And yet you *will* weep and know why.
Now no matter, child, the name:
Sórrow's spríngs áre the same.
Nor mouth had, no nor mind, expressed
What heart heard of, ghost guessed:
It ís the blight man was born for,
It is Margaret you mourn for.

WILLIAM WORDSWORTH

Lines Written in Early Spring

I heard a thousand blended notes,
While in a grove I sate reclined,
In that sweet mood when pleasant thoughts
Bring sad thoughts to the mind.

To her fair works did Nature link
The human soul that through me ran;
And much it grieved my heart to think
What man has made of man.

Through primrose tufts, in that green bower,
The periwinkle trailed its wreaths;
And 'tis my faith that every flower
Enjoys the air it breathes.

The birds around me hopped and played,
Their thoughts I cannot measure: –
But the least motion which they made,
It seemed a thrill of pleasure.

The budding twigs spread out their fan,
To catch the breezy air;
And I must think, do all I can,
That there was pleasure there.

If this belief from heaven be sent,
If such be Nature's holy plan,
Have I not reason to lament
What man has made of man?

PAUL FARLEY

Whitebeam

The sixty-miles-per-hour plants, the growth
that lines the summer corridors of sight
along our major roads, the overlooked
backdrop to 'Preston, 37 miles'.
Speed-camera foliage; the white flowers
of Mays and Junes, the scarlet fruits of autumn
lay wasted in the getting from A to B.
Hymn to forward-thinking planting schemes,
though some seem in two minds: the greenwood leaves
are white-furred, have a downy underside
as if the heartwood knew in its heart of hearts
the days among beech and oak would lead to these
single file times, these hard postings,
and civilised itself with handkerchiefs.

Binsey Poplars
felled 1879

My aspens dear, whose airy cages quelled,
Quelled or quenched in leaves the leaping sun,
All felled, felled, are all felled;
 Of a fresh and following folded rank
  Not spared, not one
  That dandled a sandalled
 Shadow that swam or sank
On meadow and river and wind-wandering weed-winding
 bank.

O if we but knew what we do
 When we delve or hew –
 Hack and rack the growing green!
  Since country is so tender
  To touch, her being só slender,
 That, like this sleek and seeing ball
 But a prick will make no eye at all,
 Where we, even where we mean
  To mend her we end her,
  When we hew or delve:
After-comers cannot guess the beauty been.
 Ten or twelve, only ten or twelve
  Strokes of havoc únselve
  The sweet especial scene,
 Rural scene, a rural scene,
 Sweet especial rural scene.

WALDO WILLIAMS

(translated by Tony Conran)

The Ancient Wood

The old wood, look, is growing again,
   On every side life is flooding back
Though it's been felled, cut down to feed inferno
   In the trenches of France for four black years.

Four hideous years of mud and bloodshed,
   Four deadly years 'mid steel and bomb,
Old years, old years to break Marged's heart,
   Years to wither the soul of Twm.

But look, the ancient wood's growing again,
   The scab is lifting cleanly from the cut . . .
Though governors of men and their inventors
   Contrive more weapons of damnation yet.

O that gentle wood, I could weep tears,
   So silly sooth your faith in human good,
Despite every grief, so eagerly awaiting
   The hour that reveals us Sons of God.

The Trees

The trees are coming into leaf
Like something almost being said;
The recent buds relax and spread,
Their greenness is a kind of grief.

Is it that they are born again
And we grow old? No, they die too.
Their yearly trick of looking new
Is written down in rings of grain.

Yet still the unresting castles thresh
In fullgrown thickness every May.
Last year is dead, they seem to say,
Begin afresh, afresh, afresh.

A. E. HOUSMAN

'Loveliest of Trees'

Loveliest of trees, the cherry now
Is hung with bloom along the bough,
And stands about the woodland ride
Wearing white for Eastertide.

Now, of my threescore years and ten,
Twenty will not come again,
And take from seventy springs a score,
It only leaves me fifty more.

And since to look at things in bloom
Fifty springs are little room,
About the woodlands I will go
To see the cherry hung with snow.

JOHN CLARE

First Sight of Spring

The hazel-blooms, in threads of crimson hue,
Peep through the swelling buds, foretelling Spring,
Ere yet a white-thorn leaf appears in view,
Or March finds throstles pleased enough to sing.
To the old touchwood tree woodpeckers cling
A moment, and their harsh-toned notes renew;
In happier mood, the stockdove claps his wing;
The squirrel sputters up the powdered oak,
With tail cocked o'er his head, and ears erect,
Startled to hear the woodman's understroke;
And with the courage which his fears collect,
He hisses fierce half malice and half glee,
Leaping from branch to branch about the tree,
In winter's foliage, moss and lichens, deckt.

JOHN CLARE

Wood Rides

Who hath not felt the influence that so calms
The weary mind in summer's sultry hours
When wandering thickest woods beneath the arms
Of ancient oaks and brushing nameless flowers
That verge the little ride? Who hath not made
A minute's waste of time and sat him down
Upon a pleasant swell to gaze awhile
On crowding ferns bluebells and hazel leaves
And showers of lady smocks so called by toil
When boys sprote-gathering sit on stulps and weave
Garlands while barkmen pill the fallen tree
– Then mid the green variety to start?
Who hath not met that mood from turmoil free
And felt a placid joy refreshed at heart?

RUDYARD KIPLING

The Way Through the Woods

They shut the road through the woods
Seventy years ago.
Weather and rain have undone it again,
And now you would never know
There was once a road through the woods
Before they planted the trees.
It is underneath the coppice and heath
And the thin anemones.
Only the keeper sees
That, where the ring-dove broods,
And the badgers roll at ease,
There was once a road through the woods.

Yet, if you enter the woods
Of a summer evening late,
When the night-air cools on the trout-ringed pools
Where the otter whistles his mate,
(They fear not men in the woods,
Because they see so few.)
You will hear the beat of a horse's feet,
And the swish of a skirt in the dew,
Steadily cantering through
The misty solitudes,
As though they perfectly knew
The old lost road through the woods. . . .
But there is no road through the woods.

DOUGLAS DUNN

Woodnotes

Looking into a wood, the mind gets lost
In complicated sameness, on and on.
Senses grow green and wooden. My own ghost
Waves from ground-misted ferns, and then it's gone
In half the time it takes to blink. Mind, leaf,
Life, mist, stop together in the soft clock
Within me, caught on thorns of disbelief
And welcome, as a life's *tick-tock, tick-tock*
Delivers its involuntary beats
Into an unthinned forest's olive light
Clammy with earth-locked rain, high summer heat's
Low airlessness, dusk dwindling into night.

A selfish, inner, pleasurable fright
Lasting no time at all, or man-shaped mist,
Botanic fog, a kind of second-sight,
A trick of light that says I, too, exist –
Whatever incommunicable threat
Stood in the ferns and waved – knowable fate,
Momento mori or my spirit's sweat
Evaporating – I saw my duplicate.
Abject but happy with the sight I saw
I stood and sniffed the stink of my remorse
Flow from my years and deeds, fault laced with flaw,
A silent, sniffing, waving, grinning discourse.

Silence like music that must not be played,
A score that must be read with the body posed
At a forbidden instrument, dismayed
Hands locked above potential music closed
To its performance – play it in the mind,
An abstract symphony releasing real
Ethical harmonies until they're signed

As what you cannot say but what you feel.
In a birdless forest where no fresh winds blow
I saw my other stand among the ferns
And what I didn't know I got to know
And what I learned is what a dead man learns.

Oblivion at an instant's open door –
The green of it, my whole life running past –
And then I was back again, the forest's floor
Greener than ever in the hemmed-in vast
Confinedness of the wood. I waved back
At where I'd been while being where
I'd seen him/me. A leaf dripped and a black
Defoliated tree creaked like my chair
But quietly so that only I could hear
(Or so I thought) its phrases of dead wood
Dismiss themselves; but what they meant was clear –
Revise your life, and use your solitude.

Exilic, but the root still strong and deep,
The feeling hurt me but a gratitude
Rose up within me and a big upsweep
Of thoughts I can't describe but wish I could.
I felt fictitious, shoved into a realm
Outside quotidian experience
For grey-green light and mist to overwhelm
In a self-haunted, near-nocturnal rinse,
As of the end of something, or of me
And what I've done, and what I do, a stop.
Cool darkness shivered in that leafless tree.
A drip formed on a fern. I watched it drop.

A tiny noise. Water descending from
One leaf to another in the laddered air
And if you listen hard there is rhythm
To this belated rain on the green stair
Down to the damp ground, and it is as if
Water is careful, and leaves are careful too,
Helping each other on the leaf-cupped cliff

That is existence, down from the high blue
Through the green, and into the supporting earth.
To work this out would show me as a fraud –
All life's design as birth, and then rebirth.
It takes more than religion to make God.

ALEXANDER POPE

from *Windsor Forest*
To *the Right Honourable George, Lord Lansdowne*

Non injussa cano: Te nostrae, *Vare*, myricae,
Te *Nemus* omne canet; nec Phoebo gratior ulla est
Quam sibi quae *Vari* praescripsit pagina nomen.

VIRGIL

Thy forests, Windsor! and thy green retreats,
At once the monarch's and the muse's seats,
Invite my lays. Be present, sylvan maids!
Unlock your springs, and open all your shades.
GRANVILLE commands; your aid, O muses, bring!
What muse for GRANVILLE can refuse to sing?
  The groves of Eden, vanished now so long,
Live in description, and look green in song:
These, were my breast inspired with equal flame,
Like them in beauty, should be like in fame.
Here hills and vales, the woodland and the plain,
Here earth and water seem to strive again,
Not chaos-like together crushed and bruised,
But, as the world, harmoniously confused:
Where order in variety we see,
And where, though all things differ, all agree.
Here waving groves a chequered scene display,
And part admit, and part exclude the day;
As some coy nymph her lover's warm address
Nor quite indulges, nor can quite repress.
There, interspersed in lawns and opening glades,
Thin trees arise that shun each other's shades.
Here in full light the russet plains extend:
There wrapped in clouds the blueish hills ascend.
Ev'n the wild heath displays her purple dyes,
And 'midst the desert fruitful fields arise,
That crowned with tufted trees and springing corn,

Like verdant isles the sable waste adorn.
Let India boast her plants, nor envy we
The weeping amber or the balmy tree,
While by our oaks the precious loads are born,
And realms commanded which those trees adorn.
Not proud Olympus yields a nobler sight,
Though Gods assembled grace his towering height,
Than what more humble mountains offer here,
Where, in their blessings, all those Gods appear.
See Pan with flocks, with fruits Pomona crowned,
Here blushing Flora paints th'enamelled ground,
Here Ceres' gifts in waving prospect stand,
And nodding tempt the joyful reaper's hand;
Rich Industry sits smiling on the plains,
And peace and plenty tell, a STUART reigns.
    Not thus the land appeared in ages past,
A dreary desert, and a gloomy waste,
To savage beasts and savage laws a prey,
And kings more furious and severe than they;
Who claimed the skies, dispeopled air and floods,
The lonely lords of empty wilds and woods:
Cities laid waste, they stormed the dens and caves,
(For wiser brutes were backward to be slaves.)
What could be free, when lawless beasts obeyed,
And ev'n the elements a tyrant swayed?
In vain kind seasons swelled the teeming grain,
Soft showers distilled, and suns grew warm in vain;
The swain with tears his frustrate labour yields,
And famished dies amidst his ripened fields.
What wonder then, a beast or subject slain
Were equal crimes in a despotic reign?
Both doomed alike, for sportive tyrants bled,
But while the subject starved, the beast was fed.
Proud Nimrod first the bloody chase began,
A mighty hunter, and his prey was man:
Our haughty Norman boasts that barbarous name,
And makes his trembling slaves the royal game.
The fields are ravished from th'industrious swains,
From men their cities, and from Gods their fanes:

The levelled towns with weeds lie covered o'er;
The hollow winds through naked temples roar;
Round broken columns clasping ivy twined;
O'er heaps of ruin stalked the stately hind;
The fox obscene to gaping tombs retires,
And savage howlings fill the sacred quires.
Awed by his nobles, by his commons cursed,
Th'oppressor ruled tyrannic where he durst,
Stretched o'er the poor and church his iron rod,
And served alike his vassals and his God.
Whom ev'n the Saxon spared and bloody Dane,
The wanton victims of his sport remain.
But see, the man who spacious regions gave
A waste for beasts, himself denied a grave!
Stretched on the lawn his second hope survey,
At once the chaser, and at once the prey:
Lo Rufus, tugging at the deadly dart,
Bleeds in the forest, like a wounded hart.
Succeeding monarchs heard the subjects' cries,
Nor saw displeased the peaceful cottage rise.
Then gathering flocks on unknown mountains fed,
O'er sandy wilds were yellow harvests spread,
The forests wondered at th' unusual grain,
And secret transport touched the conscious swain.
Fair Liberty, Britannia's Goddess, rears
Her cheerful head, and leads the golden years.

JACKIE KAY

The World of Trees
(inspired by the Forest of Burnley)

Sycamore. Mountain Ash. Beech. Birch. Oak.

In the middle of the forest the trees stood.
And the beech knew the birch was there.
And the mountain ash breathed the same air
as the sycamore, and everywhere

the wind blew, the trees understood each other:
How the river made the old oak lean to the east,
how the felled beech changed the currents of the wind,
how the two common ash formed a canapé,

and grew in a complementary way.
Between them they shared a full head of hair.
Some amber curls of the one could easily
belong to the other: twin trees, so similar.

Sycamore. Mountain Ash. Beech. Birch. Oak.

Some trees crouched in the forest waiting,
for another tree to die so that they could
shoot up suddenly in that new space;
stretch out comfortably for the blue sky.

Some trees grew mysterious mushroom fungi,
shoelace, honey, intricate as a grandmother's lace.
The wind fluttered the leaves; the leaves flapped their wings.
Birds flew from the trees. Sometimes they'd sing.

The tall trees, compassionate, understood everything:
grief – they stood stock still, branches drooped in despair.
Fear – they exposed their many roots, tugged their gold hair.
Anger – they shook in the storm, pointed their bony fingers.

Sycamore. Mountain Ash. Beech. Birch. Oak.

The trees knew each other's secrets.
In the deep green heart of the forest.
Each tree loved another tree best.
Each tree, happy to rest, lean a little to the east,

or to the west, when the moon loomed high above,
the big white eye of the woods.
And they stood together as one in the dark,
with the stars sparkling from their branches,

completely at ease, breathing in the cold night air
swishing a little in the breeze,
dreaming of glossy spring leaves
in the fine, distinguished company of trees.

Sycamore. Mountain Ash. Beech. Birch. Oak.

JOHN CLARE

In Hilly Wood

How sweet to be thus nestling deep in boughs
Upon an ashen stoven pillowing me;
Faintly are heard the ploughmen at their ploughs,
But not an eye can find its way to see.
The sunbeams scarce molest me with a smile,
So thick the leafy armies gather round;
And where they do, the breeze blows cool the while,
Their leafy shadows dancing on the ground.
Full many a flower, too, wishing to be seen,
Perks up its head the hiding grass between –
In mid-wood silence, thus, how sweet to be,
Where all the noises that on peace intrude
Come from the chittering cricket, bird and bee,
Whose songs have charms to sweeten solitude.

ALICE OSWALD

Wood Not Yet Out

closed and containing everything, the land
leaning all round to block it from the wind,
a squirrel sprinting in startles and sees
sections of distance tilted through the trees
and where you jump the fence a flap of sacking
does for a stile, you walk through webs, the cracking
bushtwigs break their secrecies, the sun
vanishes up, instantly come and gone.
once in, you hardly notice as you move,
the wood keeps lifting up its hope, I love
to stand among the last trees listening down
to the releasing branches where I've been –
the rain, thinking I've gone, crackles the air
and calls by name the leaves that aren't yet there

ELIZA KEARY

Through the Wood

Outside,
A world in sunshine;
Upon an afternoon
Once in June.
Such a wide,
Deep light-flooding, we were almost
Drowned in it where we stood,
Nellie and I; but inside the Wood
Clean stems grew close to each other; overhead
The intertwined light branches threw
Sweet shade on the rough ground.
I said, 'Nellie,
Let us walk into the tall Wood.'
She, putting her hand in mine,
Led me on softly, and so replied.
We made the only sound that there was,
With our footsteps crushing
The light tumble of leaves on scant grass;
Not the ghost of a bird's song under
Any cover of bush.
So along and along
We went, pushing
Our way where the tangled wood came,
Neither inclined for talking. As for me,
It was all I wanted, to walk by Nellie;
And she –. O! no blame
To the rapt wonder in her face.
This was Nellie –
The great silent glory
Of the beautiful day
Had found a place that he could stay
In – Nellie –
And wrote her through with his story.

So she passed on silently,
Walking by me,
Heaven's temple by me.
Heaven is full of love,
I thought, over and over,
And said to my heart, 'Hush!
You are happy, certainly.'
Just then, from above,
Came three notes of a thrush,
Satisfied, low, out of a full breast;
Then Nellie broke silence, and said,
'You know we shall part presently, you and I,
At the end of the Wood. Friend,
I've a favour to ask of you; –
I may call you friend, and won't tell
A long tale; one word's best.
This little packet – well,
Give it to Robert,
Into his own hand.
Thank you. He will understand.
I knew you wouldn't mind it for me.
You're not hurt?'
'I – Oh, no!' I understood.
After that, silently,
We walked on to the end of the Wood.

*   *   *

Outside,
A world in sunshine;
She with her hand in mine:
Such a wide, dark flood;
I died in it, where I stood –
By the side of Nellie.

Coast and Sea

MATTHEW ARNOLD

Dover Beach

The sea is calm to-night,
The tide is full, the moon lies fair
Upon the Straits; – on the French coast, the light
Gleams, and is gone; the cliffs of England stand,
Glimmering and vast, out in the tranquil bay.
Come to the window, sweet is the night air!
Only, from the long line of spray
Where the ebb meets the moon-blanch'd sand,
Listen! you hear the grating roar
Of pebbles which the waves suck back, and fling,
At their return, up the high strand,
Begin, and cease, and then again begin,
With tremulous cadence slow, and bring
The eternal note of sadness in.

    Sophocles long ago
Heard it on the Aegaean, and it brought
Into his mind the turbid ebb and flow
Of human misery; we
Find also in the sound a thought,
Hearing it by this distant northern sea.

The sea of faith
Was once, too, at the full, and round earth's shore
Lay like the folds of a bright girdle furl'd;
But now I only hear
Its melancholy, long, withdrawing roar,
Retreating to the breath
Of the night-wind down the vast edges drear
And naked shingles of the world.

Ah, love, let us be true
To one another! for the world, which seems
To lie before us like a land of dreams,
So various, so beautiful, so new,
Hath really neither joy, nor love, nor light,
Nor certitude, nor peace, nor help for pain;
And we are here as on a darkling plain
Swept with confused alarms of struggle and flight,
Where ignorant armies clash by night.

ROBERT BROWNING

Meeting at Night

I

The grey sea and the long black land;
And the yellow half-moon large and low;
And the startled little waves that leap
In fiery ringlets from their sleep,
As I gain the cove with pushing prow,
And quench its speed i' the slushy sand.

II

Then a mile of warm sea-scented beach;
Three fields to cross till a farm appears;
A tap at the pane, the quick sharp scratch
And blue spurt of a lighted match,
And a voice less loud, through its joys and fears,
Than the two hearts beating each to each!

THOMAS HARDY

Beeny Cliff

O the opal and the sapphire of that wandering western sea,
And the woman riding high above with bright hair flapping free –
The woman whom I loved so, and who loyally loved me.

The pale mews plained below us, and the waves seemed far away
In a nether sky, engrossed in saying their ceaseless babbling say,
As we laughed light-heartedly aloft on that clear-sunned March
     day.

A little cloud then cloaked us, and there flew an irised rain,
And the Atlantic dyed its levels with a dull misfeatured stain,
And then the sun burst out again, and purples prinked the main.

– Still in all its chasmal beauty bulks old Beeny to the sky,
And shall she and I not go there once again now March is nigh,
And the sweet things said in that March say anew there by and
     by?

What if still in chasmal beauty looms that wild weird western
     shore,
The woman now is – elsewhere – whom the ambling pony bore,
And nor knows nor cares for Beeny, and will laugh there
     nevermore.

THOMAS HARDY

To a Sea-Cliff
(Durlston Head)

Lend me an ear
While I read you here
A page from your history,
    Old cliff – not known
    To your solid stone,
Yet yours inseparably.

    Near to your crown
    There once sat down
A silent listless pair;
    And the sunset ended,
    And dark descended,
And still the twain sat there.

    Past your jutting head
    Then a line-ship sped,
Lit brightly as a city;
    And she sobbed: 'There goes
    A man who knows
I am his, beyond God's pity!'

    He slid apart
    Who had thought her heart
His own, and not aboard
    A bark, sea-bound . . .
    That night they found
Between them lay a sword.

CHARLOTTE SMITH

from *Beachy Head*

On thy stupendous summit, rock sublime!
That o'er the channel rear'd, half way at sea
The mariner at early morning hails,
I would recline; while Fancy should go forth,
And represent the strange and awful hour
Of vast concussion; when the Omnipotent
Stretch'd forth his arm, and rent the solid hills,
Bidding the impetuous main flood rush between
The rifted shores, and from the continent
Eternally divided this green isle.
Imperial lord of the high southern coast!
From thy projecting head-land I would mark
Far in the east the shades of night disperse,
Melting and thinned, as from the dark blue wave
Emerging, brilliant rays of arrowy light
Dart from the horizon; when the glorious sun
Just lifts above it his resplendent orb.
Advances now, with feathery silver touched,
The rippling tide of flood; glisten the sands,
While, inmates of the chalky clefts that scar
Thy sides precipitous, with shrill harsh cry,
Their white wings glancing in the level beam,
The terns, and gulls, and tarrocks, seek their food,
And thy rough hollows echo to the voice
Of the grey choughs, and ever restless daws,
With clamour, not unlike the chiding hounds,
While the lone shepherd, and his baying dog,
Drive to thy turfy crest his bleating flock.

WILLIAM SHAKESPEARE

from *King Lear, Act 4, Scene 6*

Come on, sir; here's the place. Stand still. How fearful
And dizzy 'tis to cast one's eyes so low!
The crows and choughs that wing the midway air
Show scarce so gross as beetles. Halfway down
Hangs one that gathers sampire: dreadful trade;
Methinks he seems no bigger than his head.
The fishermen that walk upon the beach
Appear like mice; and yond tall anchoring bark,
Diminished to her cock; her cock, a buoy
Almost too small for sight. The murmuring surge
That on th' unnumb'red idle pebble chafes
Cannot be heard so high. I'll look no more,
Lest my brain turn, and the deficient sight
Topple down headlong.

ANNE RIDLER

Bempton Cliffs

Strangely quiet, the cliffs are, as we approach.
The sea swallows the sound until, suddenly,
As though a door were opened into a hall
(A prayer meeting, a gaggle of gossiping talkers)
It's there, around us. And the sky in shreds
With whirling birds.

Now I am earthbound in a city of fliers,
A rooted maypole, while about my head
The dancers weave their patterns, maypole ribbons
Of varying flight, and their incessant cries
Are skeins of sound, flung up into the air.

Law rules the dance; in all these comings and goings
None is aimless. And all comparisons –
Comic, anthropomorphic – that spring to mind
At the sight of guillemots, tier upon tier
In dinner-jackets, like a festival chorus,
Are out of place.
                    Comparisons anyhow
Die in astonishment when we reach the cliff
Where the great ocean birds are perched.

That was no tractor you heard, but the gannets' talk.

The gale-masters, precipitous plungers,
Brood here on their scraps of net
With smaller birds around them. Viking beak
With its armoured look, subdued for a mating kiss,
Domestic as a farmyard goose;
So close, it seems as though a hand stretched out
Could touch and stroke the saffron head.

DAVID HARSENT

Finisterre

That slim isthmus where one sea beats on the southern shore,
another sea on the northern, is called by sailors and strangers
  Finisterre
or, sometimes, Terra Nada. It was there,
on that cold strip of rock and broom and bright rag-weed that
  four
hundred were run to ground,
motherless sons, widowers, the orphans of orphans, their gear
tossed on the tide or lost to the offshore wind.

So much for gyromancy, so much for prayer.

We went there next morning, the weather holding clear,
and made a ring, the faint-hearted hand-in-glove with the blind.
It wasn't long before one of the women claimed to hear
a difference in the gulls' cries, something raw,
full-throated, a note so thick with fear
it took her breath and brought her to her knees. The air
was full of it then – everyone heard it clear,
or said they did, and stood in awe
to be there as the legend rose and formed,
the skirl of the dead in our ears, their silt still on the sand.

ALFRED, LORD TENNYSON

'Break, Break, Break'

Break, break, break,
   On thy cold grey stones, O Sea!
And I would that my tongue could utter
   The thoughts that arise in me.

O well for the fisherman's boy,
   That he shouts with his sister at play!
O well for the sailor lad,
   That he sings in his boat on the bay!

And the stately ships go on
   To their haven under the hill;
But O for the touch of a vanish'd hand,
   And the sound of a voice that is still!

Break, break, break
   At the foot of thy crags, O Sea!
But the tender grace of a day that is dead
   Will never come back to me.

EDWARD THOMAS

The Child on the Cliff

Mother, the root of this little yellow flower
Among the stones has the taste of quinine.
Things are strange today on the cliff. The sun shines so bright,
And the grasshopper works at his sewing-machine
So hard. Here's one on my hand, mother, look;
I lie so still. There's one on your book.

But I have something to tell more strange. So leave
Your book to the grasshopper, mother dear, –
Like a green knight in a dazzling market-place, –
And listen now. Can you hear what I hear
Far out? Now and then the foam there curls
And stretches a white arm out like a girl's.

Fishes and gulls ring no bells. There cannot be
A chapel or church between here and Devon,
With fishes or gulls ringing its bell, – hark. –
Somewhere under the sea or up in heaven.
'It's the bell, my son, out in the bay
On the buoy. It does sound sweet today.'

Sweeter I never heard, mother, no, not in all Wales.
I should like to be lying under that foam,
Dead, but able to hear the sound of the bell,
And certain that you would often come
And rest, listening happily.
I should be happy if that could be.

PETER PORTER

Seahorses

When we were children
We would cheer to find a seahorse
Among the wrack the breakers lifted
On to the beach. Sometimes two or three were together,
A team to pull a chariot of cuttle,
Or like a suicide wreathed in fine
Sea ivy and bleached sea roses
One stiff but apologetic in its trance.
Seahorses were vikings;
Somewhere they impassively
Launched on garrulous currents
Seeking a far grave: wherever
That was, they set their stallion
Noses to it, ready to be garnered
In the sea's time at the sea's pleasure.

If we wondered why we loved them
We might have thought
They were the only creatures which had to die
Before we could see them—
In this early rule of death we'd recognize
The armorial pride of head, the unbending
Seriousness of small creatures,
Credit them with the sea's rare love
Which threw them to us in their beauty,
Unlike the vast and pitiable whale
Which must be quickly buried for its smell.

PHILIP LARKIN

To the Sea

To step over the low wall that divides
Road from concrete walk above the shore
Brings sharply back something known long before –
The miniature gaiety of seasides.
Everything crowds under the low horizon:
Steep beach, blue water, towels, red bathing caps,
The small hushed waves' repeated fresh collapse
Up the warm yellow sand, and further off
A white steamer stuck in the afternoon –

Still going on, all of it, still going on!
To lie, eat, sleep in hearing of the surf
(Ears to transistors, that sound tame enough
Under the sky), or gently up and down
Lead the uncertain children, frilled in white
And grasping at enormous air, or wheel
The rigid old along for them to feel
A final summer, plainly still occurs
As half an annual pleasure, half a rite,

As when, happy at being on my own,
I searched the sand for Famous Cricketers,
Or, farther back, my parents, listeners
To the same seaside quack, first became known.
Strange to it now, I watch the cloudless scene:
The same clear water over smoothed pebbles,
The distant bathers' weak protesting trebles
Down at its edge, and then the cheap cigars,
The chocolate-papers, tea-leaves, and, between

The rocks, the rusting soup-tins, till the first
Few families start the trek back to the cars.
The white steamer has gone. Like breathed-on glass
The sunlight has turned milky. If the worst
Of flawless weather is our falling short,
It may be that through habit these do best,
Coming to water clumsily undressed
Yearly; teaching their children by a sort
Of clowning; helping the old, too, as they ought.

Seascape and Single Figure

It isn't the seagulls, whitened
Lecterns of rock or wind,
Whose cries make the heart cry,
But those who scatter delinquent
Footprints, feathered with sand,
As the visible evidence that children fly.

My shadow, askance and pale,
Crosses the beach with me:
We sit on the spread towel,
Folded together complicatedly
As a marriage or Swiss Army knife.
So the shadow is one with the life.

Nearby, a village is settled
With windbreaks, push-chairs.
Children gather and build.
The candid embodiment of
The most popular version of love,
They are the day's, its flush, its goldening, theirs.

And disinheritance
Is the sea, burnt almost to nothing,
A chemical, austere,
Standoffish radiance
Sending a few thin waves, slow-lathering,
Choked, to encrust the shore.

What does it matter if less
Than a dazzled moment ago
I swam with the warmer flow?
Those choices, that lack of choice,
That enviable sorrow,
Are not renewable.

Bright as crayoned sunshine, still
The coast-train winds among
The drifted crowds, pouring them out like grain
From a summer which, for so long
Disguised as a miracle,
Empties only to fill and brim again.

(Talland Bay, Cornwall, 1972)

ANNE STEVENSON

Trinity at Low Tide

Sole to sole with your reflection
   on the glassy beach,
your shadow gliding beside you,
   you stride in triplicate across the sand.
Waves, withdrawn to limits on their leash,
   are distant, repetitious whisperings,
while doubling you, the rippling tideland deepens you.

Under you, transparent yet exact,
   your downward ghost keeps pace –
pure image, cleansed of human overtones:
   a travelling sun, your face;
your breast, a field of sparkling shells and stones.
   All blame is packed into that black, featureless
third trick of light that copies you
            and cancels you.

DANNIE ABSE

At Ogmore-by-Sea This August Evening

I think of one who loved this estuary –
my father – who, self-taught, scraped upon
an obstinate violin. Now, in a room
darker than the darkening evening outside,
I choose a solemn record, listen to
a violinist inhabit a Bach partita.
This violinist and violin are unified.

Such power! The music summons night. What more?
It's twenty minutes later into August
before the gaudy sun sinks to Australia.
Now nearer than the promontory paw
and wincing electric of Porthcawl
look! the death-boat black as anthracite,
at its spotlit prow a pale familiar.
Father? Here I am, Father. I see you
jubilantly lit, an ordered carnival.
The tide's in. From Nash Point no foghorns howl.
I'm at your favourite place where once you held
a bending rod and taught me how to bait
the ragworm hooks. Here, Father, here, tonight
we'll catch a bass or two, or dabs, or cod.

Senseless conjuration! I wipe my smile away
for now, lit at the prow, not my father
but his skeleton stands. The spotlight fails,
the occult boat's a smudge while three far lighthouses
converse in dotty exclamation marks.
The ciaccona's over, the record played,
there's nothing but the tumult of the sea.

KATHLEAN JAMIE

At Point of Ness

The golf course shifts
uneasily beside the track
where streetlight melts
to a soft frontier with winter dark.
I cross, then, helpless as a ship,
must let night load me, before
moving on between half-sensed
dry-stane walls; day-birds tucked in some nook.

Tonight, the darkness roars.
Even the fishermen's
Nissen hut seems to breathe
beside its spawn of creels,
a dreadful beaching. I walk on,
toward the shore, where night's
split open, the entire
archipelago set as sink-weight
to the sky. A wind's

caught me now; breath frosts,
and I count, to calm me, the Sound's
lighthouses as they shine and fade
across the surge. Graemsay
beams a long systolic five
to one of dark; Hoy a distant
two: two; scattered buoys
blink where skerries drown, then cut
to sea and stars, then
bloom again, weird lilies
wilt and bloom, till,
heart-scared, I have it
understood:

             never   *ever*
harm – this,
                              you never could

and run – that constant roar,
the track's black vein; toward salt
lit windows, my own door . . .

                                   Sunshine
gleams the dry-stane dykes'
lovely melanoma of lichen. A wren
flicks on a weathered post
like a dud lighter, by the track
that splits the golf course
from the town's edge to the shore,
where I walk this afternoon
for a breath of air.

ROBERT LOUIS STEVENSON

The Light-Keeper

I

The brilliant kernel of the night,
The flaming lightroom circles me:
I sit within a blaze of light
Held high above the dusky sea.
Far off the surf doth break and roar
Along bleak miles of moonlit shore,
Where through the tides the tumbling wave
Falls in an avalanche of foam
And drives its churned waters home
Up many an undercliff and cave.

The clear bell chimes: the clockworks strain,
The turning lenses flash and pass,
Frame turning within glittering frame
With frosty gleam of moving glass:
Unseen by me, each dusky hour
The sea-waves welter up the tower
Or in the ebb subside again;
And ever and anon all night,
Drawn from afar by charm of light,
A sea bird beats against the pan.

And lastly when dawn ends the night
And belts the semi-orb of sea,
The tall, pale pharos in the light
Looks white and spectral as may be.
The early ebb is out: the green
Straight belt of seaweed now is seen,
That round the basement of the tower
Marks out the interspace of tide;
And watching men are heavy-eyed,
And sleepless lips are dry and sour.

The night is over like a dream:
The sea-birds cry and dip themselves:
And in the early sunlight, steam
The newly bared and dripping shelves,
Around whose verge the glassy wave
With lisping wash is heard to lave;
While, on the white tower lifted high,
The circling lenses flash and pass
With yellow light in faded glass
And sickly shine against the sky.

II

As the steady lenses circle
With a frosty gleam of glass;
And the clear bell chimes,
And the oil brims over the lip of the burner,
Quiet and still at his desk,
The lonely Light-Keeper
Holds his vigil.

Lured from far,
The bewildered seagull beats
Dully against the lantern;
Yet he stirs not, lifts not his head
From the desk where he reads,
Lifts not his eyes to see
The chill blind circle of night
Watching him through the panes.
This is his country's guardian,
The outmost sentry of peace.
This is the man
Who gives up that is lovely in living
For the means to live.

Poetry cunningly gilds
The life of the Light-Keeper,
Held on high in the blackness
In the burning kernel of night,
The seaman sees and blesses him,

The Poet, deep in a sonnet,
Numbers his inky fingers
Fitly to praise him.
Only we behold him,
Sitting, patient and stolid,
Martyr to a salary.

MATTHEW HOLLIS

The Wash

All summer the rainfall was biblical.
Seawater, nightly, brought gifts to our door:

crab claws and hawser, a boat on the highstreet,
roads leading into the sea.

Each day the reach had been rising
and those who had seen it before

were talking of *waterslain* –
a flooding so surely as nightfall

sweeping a coastline to sea.
We filled the car with what we could:

our two cats, that pair of clocks,
heads alive with flood-lore –

who put the kerf on Friary roof,
who lost his wife but not one single book.

And, for a moment, it's upon us –

We have taken the boat to the river,
toggled a path to the edge of the water
and put down where trout shoehorn at our feet.
In this boat bellied with paintpeel and moss
I will guide us upriver, away from the flood,
with a sackful of things clutched up
in the hours at dawn.

And husbands will call to their children
to come in off the field, come in
and wash for their tea. And they'll come
mud-faced and scrambling stories
of water, great water, climbing the hill.
And wives will flight from their fishing-boats
smelling of rockwind and kelp
and stand ashen, ashen; or plashing
through rooms with sandbags and peat sod
scooping up kids from the runnels.

There will be no maps for where we are,
but a swirl of haybale, splints of timber,
cattle bloating in the current.

And later, much later,
the water will come from all sides at once
and our boat will welter and coup.

And in that moment I will hold you under.
Your face will moon from the water.

*

I have seen it inside you,
                    a cue ball

where part of your head should be.
You carry the thing sewn up in your skull,

the sound of the sea trapped in
and trickling through shunts;

if you opened your mouth
seabirds would peck out your tongue.

You have sat with a friend who has it too
in cigarette clouds and silence;
                              and yet

nothing rhymes with cancer –
and this strange company is no company at all

but a waiting room of small arrangements –
the saltings turning with the aster, samphire;

the shoals of Thief Sand, Black Buoy Knock;
the boats spilling their nets off the Staithe,

a shale of oysters, lobster pots,
mussels torn out of the creek.

Tonight I scoop you from an empty bath,
naked as whale bone

                left high on the tide,
and know by now what it is.

It's not the flood I fear but what comes after –
the endless roaming to find a home

like Shuck, the Viking dog, who beats
by legend a nightpath over these marshes

looking for a boat that's long pulled out,
to find place in the heart of nothing.

JEAN INGELOW

The High Tide on the Coast
of Lincolnshire

The old mayor climbed the belfry tower,
    The ringers ran by two, by three;
'Pull, if ye never pulled before;
    Good ringers, pull your best,' quoth he.
'Play uppe, play uppe, O Boston bells!
Ply all your changes, all your swells,
    Play uppe "The Brides of Enderby."''

Men say it was a stolen tyde –
    The Lord that sent it, He knows all;
But in myne ears doth still abide
    The message that the bells let fall:
And there was nought of strange, beside
The flights of mews and peewits pied
    By millions crouched on the old sea wall.

I sat and spun within the doore,
    My thread brake off, I raised myne eyes;
The level sun, like ruddy ore,
    Lay sinking in the barren skies,
And dark against day's golden death
She moved where Lindis wandereth,
My sonne's faire wife, Elizabeth.

'Cusha! Cusha! Cusha!' calling,
Ere the early dews were falling,
Farre away I heard her song.
'Cusha! Cusha!' all along
Where the reedy Lindis floweth,
    Floweth, floweth;
From the meads where melick groweth
Faintly came her milking song –

'Cusha! Cusha! Cusha!' calling,
'For the dews will soone be falling;
Leave your meadow grasses mellow,
    Mellow, mellow;
Quit your cowslips, cowslips yellow;
Come uppe Whitefoot, come uppe Lightfoot,
Quit the stalks of parsley hollow,
    Hollow, hollow;
Come uppe Jetty, rise and follow,
From the clovers lift your head;
Come uppe Whitefoot, come uppe Lightfoot,
Come uppe Jetty, rise and follow,
Jetty, to the milking shed.'

If it be long, ay, long ago,
    When I beginne to think howe long,
Againe I hear the Lindis flow,
    Swift as an arrowe, sharpe and strong;
And all the aire, it seemeth mee,
Bin full of floating bells (sayth shee),
That ring the tune of Enderby.

Alle fresh the level pasture lay,
    And not a shadowe mote be seene,
Save where full fyve good miles away
    The steeple towered from out the greene;
And lo! the great bell farre and wide
Was heard in all the country side
That Saturday at eventide.

The swanherds where their sedges are
    Moved on in sunset's golden breath,
The shepherde lads I heard afarre,
    And my sonne's wife, Elizabeth;
Till floating o'er the grassy sea
Came downe that kindly message free,
The 'Brides of Mavis Enderby'.

Then some looked uppe into the sky,
   And all along where Lindis flows
To where the goodly vessels lie,
   And where the lordly steeple shows.
They sayde, 'And why should this thing be?
What danger lowers by land or sea?
They ring the tune of Enderby!

'For evil news from Mablethorpe,
   Of pyrate galleys warping down;
For shippes ashore beyond the scorpe,
   They have not spared to wake the towne:
But while the west bin red to see,
And storms be none, and pyrates flee,
Why ring "The Brides of Enderby"?'

I looked without, and lo! my sonne
   Came riding downe with might and main:
He raised a shout as he drew on,
   Till all the welkin rang again,
'Elizabeth! Elizabeth!'
(A sweeter woman ne'er drew breath
Than my sonne's wife, Elizabeth.)

'The olde sea wall (he cried) is downe,
   The rising tide comes on apace,
And boats adrift in yonder towne
   Go sailing uppe the market-place.'
He shook as one that looks on death:
'God save you, mother!' straight he saith;
'Where is my wife, Elizabeth?'

'Good sonne, where Lindis winds away,
   With her two bairns I marked her long;
And ere yon bells beganne to play
   Afar I heard her milking song.'
He looked across the grassy lea,
To right, to left, 'Ho Enderby!'
They rang 'The Brides of Enderby'!

With that he cried and beat his breast;
    For, lo! along the river's bed
A mighty eygre reared his crest,
    And uppe the Lindis raging sped.
It swept with thunderous noises loud;
Shaped like a curling snow-white cloud,
Or like a demon in a shroud.

And rearing Lindis backward pressed
    Shook all her trembling bankes amaine;
Then madly at the eygre's breast
    Flung uppe her weltering walls again.
Then bankes came downe with ruin and rout –
Then beaten foam flew round about –
Then all the mighty floods were out.

So farre, so fast the eygre drave,
    The heart had hardly time to beat,
Before a shallow seething wave
    Sobbed in the grasses at oure feet:
The feet had hardly time to flee
Before it brake against the knee,
And all the world was in the sea.

Upon the roofe we sate that night,
    The noise of bells went sweeping by;
I marked the lofty beacon light
    Stream from the church tower, red and high –
A lurid mark and dread to see;
And awsome bells they were to mee,
That in the dark rang 'Enderby'.

They rang the sailor lads to guide
    From roofe to roofe who fearless rowed;
And I – my sonne was at my side,
    And yet the ruddy beacon glowed;
And yet he moaned beneath his breath,
'O come in life, or come in death!
O lost! my love, Elizabeth.'

And didst thou visit him no more?
  Thou didst, thou didst, my daughter deare;
The waters laid thee at his doore,
  Ere yet the early dawn was clear.
Thy pretty bairns in fast embrace,
The lifted sun shone on thy face,
Downe drifted to thy dwelling-place.

That flow strewed wrecks about the grass,
  That ebbe swept out the flocks to sea;
A fatal ebbe and flow, alas!
  To manye more than myne and mee:
But each will mourn his own (she saith),
And sweeter woman ne'er drew breath
Than my sonne's wife, Elizabeth.

  I shall never hear her more
  By the reedy Lindis shore,
  'Cusha! Cusha! Cusha!' calling,
  Ere the early dews be falling;
  I shall never hear her song,
  'Cusha! Cusha!' all along
  Where the sunny Lindis floweth,
      Goeth, floweth;
  From the meads where melick groweth,
  When the water winding down,
  Onward floweth to the town.

  I shall never see her more
  Where the reeds and rushes quiver,
      Shiver, quiver;
  Stand beside the sobbing river,
  Sobbing, throbbing, in its falling
  To the sandy lonesome shore;
  I shall never hear her calling,
  Leave your meadow grasses mellow,
      Mellow, mellow;
  Quit your cowslips, cowslips yellow;
  Come uppe Whitefoot, come uppe Lightfoot;

Quit your pipes of parsley hollow,
    Hollow, hollow;
Come uppe Lightfoot, rise and follow;
    Lightfoot, Whitefoot,
From your clovers lift the head;
Come uppe Jetty, follow, follow,
Jetty, to the milking shed.

ANNE RIDLER

Zennor

Seen from these cliffs the sea circles slowly.
    Ponderous and blue today, with waves furled,
    Slowly it crosses the curved world.
We wind in its waters with the tide,
    But the pendent ships afar
    Where the lightest blue and low clouds are
We lose as they hover and over the horizon slide.

When it was a dark blue heaven with foam like stars
    We saw it lean above us from the shore,
    And over the rocks the waves rear
Immense, and coming in with crests on fire;
    We could not understand,
    Finding the sea so high above the land,
What held its waters from flooding the world entire.

Today it lies in place, and the dun houses,
    The apple-green cloudy oats, the cows that seem
    Compact of the yellow crust of their cream,
Shrink on Amalveor's grey and tawny sides,
    Sucking the last shreds of sun.
    But all life here is carried on
Against the crash and cry of the moving tides.

GERARD MANLEY HOPKINS

The Sea and the Skylark

On ear and ear two noises too old to end
  Trench – right, the tide that ramps against the shore;
  With a flood or a fall, low lull-off or all roar,
Frequenting there while moon shall wear and wend.

Left hand, off land, I hear the lark ascend,
  His rash-fresh re-winded new-skbeinèd score
  In crisps of curl off wild winch whirl, and pour
And pelt music, till none's to spill nor spend.

How these two shame this shallow and frail town!
  How ring right out our sordid turbid time,
Being pure! We, life's pride and cared-for crown,

  Have lost that cheer and charm of earth's past prime:
Our make and making break, are breaking, down
  To man's last dust, drain fast towards man's first slime.

TED HUGHES

Crow on the Beach

Hearing shingle explode, seeing it skip,
Crow sucked his tongue.
Seeing sea-grey mash a mountain of itself
Crow tightened his goose-pimples.
Feeling spray from the sea's root nothinged on his crest
Crow's toes gripped the wet pebbles.
When the smell of the whale's den, the gulfing of the crab's
    last prayer,
Gimletted in his nostril
He grasped he was on earth.
                            He knew he grasped
Something fleeting
Of the sea's ogreish outcry and convulsion.
He knew he was the wrong listener unwanted
To understand or help –

His utmost gaping of brain in his tiny skull
Was just enough to wonder, about the sea,

What could be hurting so much?

NORMAN NICHOLSON

Sea to the West

When the sea's to the west
The evenings are one dazzle –
You can find no sign of water.
Sun upflows the horizon;
Waves of shine
Heave, crest, fracture,
Explode on the shore;
The wide day burns
In the incandescent mantle of the air.

Once, fifteen,
I would lean on handlebars,
Staring into the flare,
Blinded by looking,
Letting the gutterings and sykes of light
Flood into my skull.

Then, on the stroke of bedtime,
I'd turn to the town,
Cycle past purpling dykes
To a brown drizzle
Where black-scum shadows
Stagnated between backyard walls.
I pulled the warm dark over my head
Like an eiderdown.

Yet in that final stare when I
(Five times, perhaps, fifteen)
Creak protesting away –
The sea to the west,
The land darkening –
Let my eyes at the last be blinded
Not by the dark
But by dazzle.

JOHN BETJEMAN

Winter Seascape

The sea runs back against itself
  With scarcely time for breaking wave
To cannonade a slatey shelf
  And thunder under in a cave

Before the next can fully burst,
  The headwind, blowing harder still,
Smooths it to what it was at first –
  A slowly rolling water hill.

Against the breeze the breakers haste,
  Against the tide their ridges run
And all the sea's a dappled waste
  Criss-crossing underneath the sun.

Far down the beach the ripples drag
  Blown backward, rearing from the shore,
And wailing gull and shrieking shag
  Alone can pierce the ocean roar.

Unheard, a mongrel hound gives tongue,
  Unheard are shouts of little boys:
What chance has any inland lung
  Against this multi-water noise?

Here where the cliffs alone prevail
  I stand exultant, neutral, free,
And from the cushion of the gale
  Behold a huge consoling sea.

FRANCES CORNFORD

The Coast: Norfolk

As on the highway's quiet edge
He mows the grass beside the hedge,
The old man has for company
The distant, grey, salt-smelling sea,
A poppied field, a cow and calf,
The finches on the telegraph.

Across his faded back a hone,
He slowly, slowly scythes alone
In silence of the wind-soft air,
With ladies' bedstraw everywhere,
With whitened corn, and tarry poles,
And far-off gulls like risen souls.

MARGARET CAVENDISH, DUCHESS OF NEWCASTLE

Similizing the Sea to Meadowes, and Pastures, the Marriners to Shepheards, the Mast to a May-pole, Fishes to Beasts

The *Waves* like *Ridges* of *Plow'd-land* lies high,
Whereat the *Ship* doth stumble, downe doth lye.
But in a *Calme*, levell as *Meadowes* seem,
And by its *Saltnesse* makes it look as green.
When *Ships* thereon a slow, soft pace they walke,
Then *Mariners*, as *Shepheards* sing, and talke.
Some whistle, and some on their *Pipes* do play,
Thus merrily will passe their time away.
And every *Mast* is like a *May-pole* high,
Round which they dance, though not so merrily,
As *Shepheards* do, when they their *Lasses* bring,
Whereon are *Garlands* tied with *Silken string*.
But on their *Mast*, instead of *Garlands*, hung
Huge *Sailes*, and *Ropes* to tye those *Garlands* on.
Instead of *Lasses* they do dance with *Death*,
And for their *Musick* they have *Boreas Breath*.
Instead of *Wine*, and *Wassals*, drink salt *Teares*,
And for their *Meat* they feed on nought but *Feares*.
For *Flocks* of *Sheep* great sholes of *Herrings* swim,
As ravenous *Wolves* the *Whales* do feed on them.
As sportfull *Kids* skip over *Hillocks* green,
So dancing *Dolphines* on the *Waves* are seen.
The *Porpoyse*, like their watchfull *Dog* espies,
And gives them warning when great *Windes* will rise.
Instead of *Barking*, he his *Head* wil shew
Above the waters, where they rough do flow.
When showring *Raines* power downe, and *Windes* do blow:
Then fast *Men* run for *Shelter* to a *Tree*;
So *Ships* at *Anchor* lye upon the *Sea*.

DALJIT NAGRA

Look We Have Coming to Dover!

'So various, so beautiful, so new . . .'
MATTHEW ARNOLD, 'Dover Beach'

Stowed in the sea to invade
the alfresco lash of a diesel-breeze
ratcheting speed into the tide, brunt with
gobfuls of surf phlegmed by cushy come-and-go
tourists prow'd on the cruisers, lording the ministered waves.

Seagull and shoal life
vexing their blarnies upon our huddled
camouflage past the vast crumble of scummed
cliffs, scramming on mulch as thunder unbladders
yobbish rain and wind on our escape hutched in a Bedford van.

Seasons or years we reap
inland, unclocked by the national eye
or stabs in the back, teemed for breathing
sweeps of grass through the whistling asthma of parks,
burdened, ennobled – poling sparks across pylon and pylon.

Swarms of us, grafting in
the black within shot of the moon's
spotlight, banking on the miracle of sun –
span its rainbow, passport us to life. Only then
can it be human to hoick ourselves, bare-faced for the clear.

Imagine my love and I,
our sundry others, Blair'd in the cash
of our beeswax'd cars, our crash clothes, free,
we raise our charged glasses over unparasol'd tables
East, babbling our lingoes, flecked by the chalk of Britannia!

U. A. FANTHORPE

Sunderland Point and Ribchester

Sunderland Point, where sea, wind, sky
Dispute dominion, on a spur of land
So bitter that you'd think no one would take
The trouble to go there.
                                Here SAMBO lies,
A faithful NEGRO, who (attending his Mafter
From the Weft Indies) DIED
On his Arrival at Sunderland.

It is, of course, unconsecrated ground.

Now children stagger here on pilgrimage,
Their offerings the sort of things you'd find
On a pet's grave: a cross of driftwood, lashed
With binder-twine; a Woolworth vase,
Chocked up with grit and pebbles, crammed
With dead wild flowers.
                                Sam lies very low.
You can allow him any voice you like.
Despair, pneumonia, exile, love, are variously
Thought to have killed him. A good place
To bring the kids in summer at weekends.

Ribchester had a stone, now lost.
Camden preserved the proper idiom:
By this earth is covered she who was once
Aelia Matrona, who lived 28 years, 2 months,
And 8 days, and Marcus Julius Maximus,
Her son, who lived 6 years, 3 months,
And 20 days.
                                A place to bring the kids.

Children are the most authentic
Pilgrims, having farthest to go, and knowing
Least the way.
                    The Romans understood
The use and pathos of arithmetic.

And the Ribble bites its banks, and the sea gnaws at the
    shore.
So many patterns gone, the *faithful slave*, the *son*
Most dutiful to his father. The word
Strives to be faithful, but the elements
Are against it.
                    We are all exiles, Sam,
From the almost-forgotten country
Before the divorce, before the failed exam,
Before the accident, before the white man came.
Your situation's more extreme than most,
But we all of us, all of us seek
That country. And you, who so clearly were not
Your own man, lying in no man's land,
A journey's end for children, seem in your muteness
To be meaning something.
Alternative:
The massive Roman formulas: *the century*
Of Titius built 27 feet . . .
. . . According to the reply of the god.

SHEENAGH PUGH

Fixed
Anthony Gormley's Another Place: *Crosby Beach, April 2007*

Built on sand, anchored
for good, they gaze out

west across the sea
where they should have gone.

Born to be travellers,
they have left gaps

in the skylines of Cuxhaven,
De Panne, Stavanger,

where folk came to know them,
then let them go.

Now, on this beach
like any other,

words like *home* and *always*
ambush them, pin them down.

They should have unpacked
in New York, but love

holds them back, demanding
no less than possession,

cancelling their passports,
giving them a space

to call their own, whose guesthouse
was the world. Suffering

attention like some pet animal,
fond hands stroking their flanks,

they stare past love, eyes
fixed on distance.

MENNA ELFYN
(translated by Elin ap Hywel)

Seeing the Sea

To be first to see the sea
Is the closest we may ever come
To open-eyed discovery.

There she lies, a temple
helping us draw the line
between heaven and earth,
nothing and oceans.

We travel gladly towards her laughter
reaching the skirt-hem of her stories,
where her tongues tell truths.

For a time, we stare, not understanding
her depths, this divinity who will
not reveal herself, hugging her secret

and see, anew, that a sea
is no less beautiful because ships
founder on rocks, because, look,
in her split-second waves

we grow younger with each frisson;
seeing the sea
for the first time
is the closest we may come
to the wonder of eyes opened.

SAMUEL TAYLOR COLERIDGE

On Revisiting the Sea-Shore
After Long Absence, Under Strong Medical
Recommendation Not To Bathe

God be with thee, gladsome Ocean!
　How gladly greet I thee once more!
Ships and waves, and ceaseless motion,
　And men rejoicing on thy shore.

Dissuading spake the mild physician,
　'Those briny waves for thee are death!'
But my soul fulfilled her mission,
　And lo! I breathe untroubled breath!

Fashion's pining sons and daughters,
　That seek the crowd they seem to fly,
Trembling they approach thy waters;
　And what cares Nature, if they die?

Me a thousand hopes and pleasures,
　A thousand recollections bland,
Thoughts sublime, and stately measures,
　Revisit on thy echoing strand:

Dreams (the soul herself forsaking),
　Tearful raptures, boyish mirth;
Silent adorations, making
　A blessed shadow of this Earth!

O ye hopes, that stir within me,
　Health comes with you from above!
God is with me, God is in me!
　I cannot die, if Life be Love.

JOHN KEATS

On the Sea

It keeps eternal whisperings around
   Desolate shores, and with its mighty swell
   Gluts twice ten thousand caverns, till the spell
Of Hecate leaves them their old shadowy sound.
Often 'tis in such gentle temper found,
   That scarcely will the very smallest shell
   Be moved for days from where it sometime fell,
When last the winds of Heaven were unbound.
Oh ye! who have your eye-balls vexed and tired,
   Feast them upon the wideness of the Sea –
      Oh ye! whose ears are dinned with uproar rude,
   Or fed too much with cloying melody –
      Sit ye near some old cavern's mouth and brood
Until ye start, as if the sea-nymphs quired!

ROBERT GRAVES

Welsh Incident

'But that was nothing to what things came out
From the sea-caves of Criccieth yonder.'
'What were they? Mermaids? dragons? ghosts?'
'Nothing at all of any things like that.'
'What were they, then?'
                              'All sorts of queer things,
Things never seen or heard or written about,
Very strange, un-Welsh, utterly peculiar
Things. Oh, solid enough they seemed to touch,
Had anyone dared it. Marvellous creation,
All various shapes and sizes, and no sizes,
All new, each perfectly unlike his neighbour,
Though all came moving slowly out together.'
'Describe just one of them.'
                              'I am unable.'
'What were their colours?'
                              'Mostly nameless colours,
Colours you'd like to see; but one was puce
Or perhaps more like crimson, but not purplish.
Some had no colour.'
                              'Tell me, had they legs?'
'Not a leg nor foot among them that I saw.'
'But did these things come out in any order?
What o'clock was it? What was the day of the week?
Who else was present? How was the weather?'
'I was coming to that. It was half-past three
On Easter Tuesday last. The sun was shining.
The Harlech Silver Band played *Marchog Jesu*
On thirty-seven shimmering instruments,
Collecting for Caernarvon's (Fever) Hospital Fund.
The populations of Pwllheli, Criccieth,
Portmadoc, Borth, Tremadoc, Penrhyndeudraeth,
Were all assembled. Criccieth's mayor addressed them

First in good Welsh and then in fluent English,
Twisting his fingers in his chain of office,
Welcoming the things. They came out on the sand,
Not keeping time to the band, moving seaward
Silently at a snail's pace. But at last
The most odd, indescribable thing of all,
Which hardly one man there could see for wonder,
Did something recognizably a something.'
'Well, what?'
        'It made a noise.'
                'A frightening noise?'
'No, no.'
      'A musical noise? A noise of scuffling?'
'No, but a very loud, respectable noise –
Like groaning to oneself on Sunday morning
In Chapel, close before the second psalm.'
'What did the mayor do?'
             'I was coming to that.'

Surfers

September evenings they are here after work,
The light banished from the sky behind,
An industrial sunset oiling the sea.
I watch them emerge from the last wave,
Young men and girls grinning like dolphins
In their rubbers, surf-riders swept
Suddenly onto this table of dark sand
And thrift, the coastline's low moraine.

And back again to the conflict with water,
Wiping salt-stiffened hair from their eyes,
The flimsy boards pitching like driftwood
On the swell, flattening with the ebb.
Theirs, briefly, is a perilous excitement
When the current lifts them high
And they stand erect on roofs of water,
Balanced on the summit of a wave.

And there they glide, untouchable,
The moment of flight and their bodies'
Instinctive mastery lasting until
They are somersaulted into the foam
And they creep to shore exhausted,
Barefoot, wincing with the discriminate
Steps of thieves, aware perhaps
Of something they might have won, or stolen.

ALICE OSWALD

from *Dart*

I steer my wave-ski into caves
horrible to enter alone
The fur, the hair, the fingernails, the bones.

Flick out the torch, the only thread between down here and
    daylight
and count five while the sea suckles and settles.
Self-maker, speaking its meaning over mine.

At low water
I swim up a dog-leg bend into the cliff,
the tide slooshes me almost to the roof

and float inwards into the trembling sphere
of one freshwater drip drip drip
where my name disappears and the sea slides in to replace it.

There the musky fishy genital smell
of things not yet actual: shivering impulses, shadows,
    propensities,
little amorous movements, quicksilver strainings and restrainings:

each winter they gather here,
twenty seals in this room behind the sea, all swaddled
and tucked in fat, like the soul in its cylinder of flesh.

With their grandmother mouths, with their dog-soft eyes, asking
who's this moving in the dark? Me.
This is me, anonymous, water's soliloquy,

all names, all voices, Slip-Shape, this is Proteus,
whoever that is, the shepherd of the seals,
driving my many selves from cave to cave . . .

R. S. THOMAS

The Moon in Lleyn

The last quarter of the moon
of Jesus gives way
to the dark; the serpent
digests the egg. Here
on my knees in this stone
church, that is full only
of the silent congregation
of shadows and the sea's
sound, it is easy to believe
Yeats was right. Just as though
choirs had not sung, shells
have swallowed them; the tide laps
at the Bible; the bell fetches
no people to the brittle miracle
of the bread. The sand is waiting
for the running back of the grains
in the wall into its blond
glass. Religion is over, and
what will emerge from the body
of the new moon, no one
can say.
                    But a voice sounds
in my ear: Why so fast,
mortal? These very seas
are baptised. The parish
has a saint's name time cannot
unfrock. In cities that
have outgrown their promise people
are becoming pilgrims
again, if not to this place,

then to the recreation of it
in their own spirits. You must remain
kneeling. Even as this moon
making its way through the earth's
cumbersome shadow, prayer, too,
has its phases.

Copyright Acknowledgements

331

'17.14 Out of Newcastle' and 'Trinity at Low Tide' from *Poems 1955–2005* by Anne Stevenson (Bloodaxe Books, 2005) reprinted by permission of the publisher.

'Poem in October' from *Dylan Thomas: The Poems* (J. M. Dent, 1971) reprinted by permission of David Higham Associates Ltd as agents for the Trustees of the Copyrights of Dylan Thomas.

'The Village', 'The Moor', 'A Peasant', 'Islandmen' and 'The Moon in Lleyn' from *Collected Poems 1945–1990* (J. M. Dent, 1993) reprinted by permission of Phoenix Press, a division of The Orion Publishing Group.

'The Second Island' from *Plundering the Harp: Collected Poems 1940–1980* by Derick Thomson/Ruaraidh MacThòmais (Macdonald Publishers, 1982) reprinted by permission of the author.

'On Weun Cas' Mael' and 'The Ancient Wood' from *Peacemakers: Selected Poems* by Waldo Williams, translated by Tony Conran (Gomer, 1997) reprinted by permission of the publisher.

Every effort has been made to trace and contact the copyright-holders prior to publication. If notified, the publisher undertakes to rectify any errors or omissions at the earliest opportunity.

Index of Poets

Index of Poems and First Lines